LANDSCAPING
MAKES CENTS

LANDSCAPING MAKES CENTS

SMART INVESTMENTS THAT INCREASE YOUR PROPERTY VALUE

Frederick C. Campbell
and
Richard L. Dubé

A Storey Publishing Book

Storey Communications, Inc.
Schoolhouse Road
Pownal, Vermont 05261

The mission of Storey Communications
is to serve our customers by publishing practical information
that encourages personal independence in harmony with the environment.

Edited by Deborah L. Balmuth and Sarah Novak
Cover design by Meredith Maker
Cover photograph © 1996 by Jerry Howard, Positive Images
Text design and production by Susan B. Bernier
Line drawings by Carolyn Bucha
Indexed by Northwind Editorial Services

The information in this book is true and complete to the best of our knowledge. All recommendations are made without guarantee on the part of the authors or Storey Communications, Inc. The authors and publisher disclaim any liability in connection with the use of this information. For additional information please contact Storey Communications, Inc., Schoolhouse Road, Pownal, Vermont 05261.

Storey Publishing books are available for special premium and promotional uses and for customized editions. For further information, please call the Custom Publishing Department at 800-793-9396.

Printed in the United States by Vicks Lithograph
10 9 8 7 6 5 4 3 2 1

Library of Congress Cataloging-in-Publication Data

Dubé, Richard L.
    Landscaping makes cents : smart investments that increase your property value /
  Richard L. Dubé and Federick C. Campbell.
      p.   cm.
    "A Storey Publishing book."
    Includes index.
    ISBN 0-88266-948-6 (pb. : alk. paper)
    1. Landscape gardening.   2. Landscape gardening—Economic aspects.
  3. Real property—Valuation.   4. Added value.   I. Campbell, Rick.   II. Title.
SB473.D75   1997
712'.6—dc20   96-30159
                                                           CIP

Contents

Introduction

In the last recession people found out how difficult it can be to sell a home in a down market. Many of these people also discovered that a well-landscaped home sold faster and for more money.

— Pat Baldwin, Realtor and Million Dollar Club member

YOUR HOME CAN BE A BEAUTIFUL PLACE TO live *and* can accumulate more value every year. With *Landscaping Makes Cents,* you will learn how to attain both a more livable and a more marketable home. We offer tips and instructions on how to increase the resale value of your home and make it more attractive to potential buyers. In addition, we tell you how you can save hundreds, even thousands, of dollars in this process. When you know the right questions to ask a potential contractor, designer, or nurseryperson, you've got a ticket to the best show in town — your landscape.

Landscaping Makes Cents is, in essence, an advocacy book for consumers of landscape goods and services. By reading and using this book, you will learn what goods and services you should (and should not) be purchasing and where you should (or should not) be purchasing them. All too often, landscaping contractors and consultants are called in to correct the mistakes made by uninformed, uncaring, or — worst of all — unscrupulous contractors who have taken unsuspecting homeowners for a ride. Since most homeowners often don't know any better, it's like the first ride of the season in a convertible with the top down on a sunny day. It's great while you're moving, but when you stop you could find that you're sunburned. In most cases, the contractor is ignorant of his or her complicity in your predicament.

By being better informed, you may actually help your contractor understand the impact that decisions can have on your landscape. You must know how valuable your landscape is and, as it matures, that it is very likely to grow in value beyond the money you spend. This is, of course, provided that it is done correctly. The money you spend for the right tree, planted in the right place, will grow as the tree grows!

After years as landscape professionals, we can answer your toughest landscape questions. We want to be sure you are represented by a professional. Even though we're not there in person, we can pass on our years of accumulated knowledge to you. We want you to be able to recognize the professional and to show the fraud the road. Let them take the ride, not you!

How to Use This Book

In the first section of this book, "Money *Does* Grow on Trees: Increasing Your Property Value," we look at how value is often perceived. We then explore ways that you may be able to quantify in dollars and cents the value of a beautiful landscape, and the various ways that value can actually be attributed to trees and landscapes. It's surprising to see how many different values may be assigned to a particular tree depending on its circumstances and the valuation approach. We also look at the particular concerns you should have depending on whether you are building, buying, or selling a house. If you are selling your home, you will be able to tap into your landscape's earning potential. If you are buying a home, our book will give you the confidence that you need to understand the home landscape's intrinsic value. And, if you are

building a home, you will know what it is you need to do in order to have a successful landscape without suffering consequences down the road.

The second section, "Where Do I Start? Developing a Budget and a Plan," takes you step by step through the process of setting a realistic budget that will maximize the return on your investment; determining what design elements you want and need (with a series of decision-making exercises) and which of those will add the most value to the space; and thoroughly understanding the options and approaches open to you in a wide range of softscaping (plants) and hardscaping components — how to use each element most effectively, what's involved in installing it, and money-saving tips. You will also learn about opportunities for reducing the costs of maintenance in your landsape while at the same time becoming more environmentally friendly.

The third section, "I Can't Do It All Myself: Hiring Landscape Contractors," tells you how to choose a qualified landscape contractor, and what questions you should be asking about different landscaping situations (as well as some hints and advice about the answers you should be looking for). You will also find a guide to understanding contracts and the options you have if there is a problem.

PART I

Money *Does* Grow on Trees

Increasing Your Property Value

I

The Perceived Value of Landscaping

~

WHEN WE LOOK AT A BEAUTIFUL LANDSCAPE around someone's house (maybe even your own house), we know that it has value. That is to say, there is a price someone is willing to pay to have that landscape. The question is not so much whether a good landscape *has* value as it is; the question is just *how* valuable it is. The problem in determining this is that many factors can influence the "dollar value." One of the most important of these factors is the so-called "perception of value," which varies widely from one person to the next. To understand how value can be perceived dramatically differently by different people, consider the following scenario.

■　　■　　■

You have just purchased a painting at a garage sale for $20 because you like it. You take it to a frame shop for cleaning and reframing. The framer asks you if you'd like to sell it for $50. You say, "Sure!" because you'll make a $30 profit. He takes it to an art dealer who's familiar with this particular artist and is offered $200. The framer agrees and pockets $150. The art dealer takes it to an auction house and is told that they'll give him $2,000 for it. He accepts and walks away with $1,800 to his credit. The auctioneer holds an auction and invites people who are likely to be collectors of this particular artist. He sells the painting for $25,000. It is still the same $20 painting that you purchased at the garage sale, but each subsequent owner had a different perceived value.

■　　■　　■

How much would you say a tulip bulb could be worth? You can buy a typical tulip today for about 29 cents. But in the late 17th century, in Holland, there was a time when a single tulip sold for tens of thousands of dollars. The skyrocketing prices of tulips during this period of "tulipomania" were a result of considerable speculation on rare breeds — streaked or variegated forms were the most popular. Values eventually plummeted, however, causing many speculators to lose vast estates and fortunes.

Today, land valuations in many places throughout the world are undergoing a similar skyrocketing increase. Probably the most outstanding example is land in downtown Tokyo, Japan. In 1992, a single square foot of ground was valued at more than $100,000. Such extremes in perceived value of land can be very dangerous, since other transactions and investments are built around the collective opinion or belief that the land is worth the amount of money stated, and that prospective buyers would gladly pay that amount.

For instance, consider the implications of a downtown Tokyo landowner using the "value" of his land as collateral on an advance from his banker to purchase a company. If, for some reason, people began to question the value of the land and say, "Wait a minute. This is ridiculous; land isn't worth anywhere near that amount of money," what do you think would happen? Since the value of the land was used to establish his collateral for the acquisition of a business and other real property, the bank could foreclose on the loan in order to replace the value of the land with cash. If you consider that there are many individuals in the same financial boat, the devaluation of the land could have a catastrophic economic effect. The basic problem is *perceived value is primarily a subjective opinion*. This subjective opinion is reinforced when a large percentage of the population agrees with it, thus giving the perceived value a greater degree of stability and making an investment based on this value more secure.

How Value Changes Over Time

Part of the problem with construction and most "built" items is that they depreciate in value. A good example is your automobile. As soon as you drive it off the car lot, it's no longer valued at the price that you paid. The rate of depreciation and loss of value is often determined by the perception and belief of the buying public.

If you buy a Ford Escort and sell it five years later, what percentage of your purchase price do you retrieve? (A 1991 Ford Escort LX cost around $12,000; the resale value in 1996 was assessed at $4,800, or 40 percent.) On the other hand, if you had purchased a Nissan Stanza, how much higher is the resale value as a percent of original cost to you? (In 1991, this car cost around $13,000; the 1996 retail is $7,575, or 58 percent.) The Nissan has a track record of higher quality than the Escort, which is reflected in its rate of depreciation.

Unlike cars, properly maintained buildings and real estate have traditionally risen in value (relative to inflation) over a period of time. However, the opposite may be true during recessions and hard times (see box on page 5).

The Value of Landscaping

How does landscaping affect the perceived value of the land? Like the land itself, landscaping generally does not decrease or depreciate in value, but gains in value over time. Landscaping does offer a distinct benefit over land or house value in that it appreciates in value simply by existing over time — that is, after you put plants in the ground, they grow (provided they are put in the right place and are maintained). A tree installed as a sapling will in time have a girth of several feet with no extra effort on the part of the homeowner. Whereas a house, if left alone, will fall into disrepair and is likely to become less valuable.

For a landscape to be valuable, it needs to be what we would call a "good landscape," which might be defined as "an attractive placement of functional and aesthetic elements." The landscape's plan and installation must be of high quality; the landscape must blend harmoniously with the architectural style of the buildings on the property to create a cohesive whole.

Some subjective terms are used here, namely, "attractive" and "high quality." What may be considered attractive to one person may or may not be so to someone else (see chapter 6). To paraphrase a famous quotation: "I can't define *attractive*, but I know it when I see it." *Quality*, on the other hand, can be defined objectively as the degree of professionalism with which a task is carried out. There is a subjective aspect of quality, however, that involves the experience, criteria, and expectations of the individual who receives the goods or services. If that person has little experience and is generally not aware of the degree of professionalism to be expected, the expectations for the outcome of a given project may be lower.

Reasons for Poor Landscaping

Would you say that most landscapes are good? Take a drive through the neighborhoods in your town and pay close attention to the landscapes. Most attempts at landscaping in the United States follow a familiar pattern — a style known as "foundation planting." This style became popular in the early 20th century when the typical new home being built had a visible foundation of three to four feet, and needed to be hidden. On houses being built today only about 6 inches of the foundation is generally visible, but the foundation planting style continues to be predominantly used. It's what our parents did and what our neighbors do, so we do it as well, even though its original purpose is no longer served. Sometimes we lose track of the original purpose of an action and just repeat it out of habit. In landscaping, habit can lead to poor practices.

Another reason for poor landscaping is that there is no license required to be a landscaper — some plants, a shovel, and a wheelbarrow can put anyone in business. The local plant nursery or garden center doesn't ask the person who buys plants for proof of competency. The creation of a good landscape requires knowledge and skills in horticulture, engineering, design, masonry, and carpentry, but there is no prerequisite for anyone performing landscape services to possess this background.

The Worth Added by Good Landscaping

For perspective from someone with a finger on the pulse of fluctuating property values, we interviewed a Million Dollar Club Realtor, Patrick Baldwin. He answered our questions as follows:

Q: Does beautiful landscaping add to the appeal of a house?

A: *Yes, it shows that the people living there have not only cared for their yard, but also for their home.*

Q: What is the difference in sales price between a well-landscaped house and an unlandscaped house?

A: *The landscaped home has a higher asking price and gets sold. The other either doesn't get sold, or is severely discounted.*

Q: When assessing the price of a house, what effect does the curb appeal have on that price? (*Curb appeal* describes the immediate positive reaction the look of the house and the landscaping creates in prospective buyers — their first impression as they pull up to the curb in front of the house.)

Landscaping is a great way to increase the property value of a new house without any surrounding plants (A). Planting directly around the house's foundation is a predominant style, often used out of habit more than aesthetic appeal (B). The best home landscaping designs blend harmoniously with the architectural style of the house and create a sense of the property as a cohesive entity (C).

A: *It attracts buyers and gets them into the house. You can't sell the house if you don't show it. Houses with good curb appeal are often landscaped for privacy. This is important to many buyers now. Corner lots used to be very popular because people liked to watch what was going on. Now those lots are less popular because people enjoy their privacy.*

Q: When assessing a house, what effect does curb appeal have on how quickly it sells?

A: *It definitely sells more quickly. Many times houses are put into color catalogs and shown to potential buyers. If a house stands out, it will be noticed and consequently sell faster.*

Q: When assessing a house, what effect does a user-friendly backyard have on the price and how quickly it sells?

A: *People seem to like decks, patios, and having the outdoors accessible for barbecues and family functions. They also enjoy privacy and something nice to look at when they're inside. If a house has accomplished this, then the perceived value goes up significantly.*

Landscaping can help make your home a dramatic focal point of the property. This generates a good first impression, or "curb appeal," that invites prospective buyers to visit.

A TESTIMONIAL ON THE VALUE OF GOOD LANDSCAPING

In 1983, I bought a house in a developing neighborhood. It came with a poorly installed lawn, which the developer considered to be "landscaping." But, as I saw it, there was a serious landscaping problem: The house looked awkwardly out of place in the yard and — worse — it looked like everyone else's house in the development.

To distinguish my house, I planted some shrubs around the foundation, put in a hedge of lilacs, built a small stone wall, planted a small perennial bed, built a flagstone walk (about 30 feet), put in a basketball hoop (the house came with a paved driveway), established a vegetable garden, and limed and fertilized the lawn. All this work took me four weekends to accomplish, and cost just a little over $900. I also added a laundry room, and paneled and carpeted the basement, at a cost of $1,250.

I lived in this house for two years. When I was ready to sell it, there were four other houses in the same development for sale with asking prices that were, on average, $6,500 less than mine. In less than two months, I sold the house for $10,000 more than I had paid for it — and the other four homes were still for sale. One of the major points of sale, as indicated by the buyers, was the landscape.

— Frederick C. Campbell

Q: When is the best time of the year to sell a home?

A: *It depends on where you live. Here in the Northeast, house sales typically peak in June, when landscaping is at its peak, and are also strong in the fall. If you must sell in the off-season, be sure to have pictures available of the landscaping at its best. More and more buyers are demanding landscaped homes. Unlandscaped or poorly landscaped homes end up being discounted and remain on the market longer. A well-landscaped, ready-to-move-into, and easily maintained house and yard have a big advantage.*

The value of a particular landscape is ultimately in the eyes of the beholders — those who are spending their time and enjoying their recreation there. However, there are certain elements that most people find appealing and valuable to have in their home landscape, as listed below. These are discussed in more detail in chapter 6.

Most Commonly Valued Elements in a Home Landscape

- Annual flowers
- Arbor/pergola
- Birdhouse/bird feeder
- Deck
- Drainage
- Dust-reducing elements
- Fall color
- Fences
- Foundation plantings
- Fragrance
- Garages
- Garden bench
- Good view of house from street
- Ground cover
- Hot tub/Jacuzzi
- Lawn
- Lighting
- Low-maintenance garden
- Parking
- Patio
- Porch
- Shade trees
- Spring-flowering bulbs
- Stone walls
- Storage shed
- Swimming pool
- Vistas
- Walkways
- Windbreaks

There is no doubt that good landscaping adds to the resale value of your home. It also increases your comfort and quality of life while you're living there. Chapter 2 describes how the value of aesthetics or beauty can be quantified and applied to landscaping, and how landscaping aesthetics can increase the overall assessed value of your property.

2

How Much Is an Aesthetically Pleasing Landscape Worth?

IN THE REAL ESTATE WORLD THE MOTTO IS, "There are three important things to have in any property you are trying to sell: location, location, and location!" The location referred to, of course, is the physical location of the site. To illustrate the truth of this motto, consider the following example.

■ ■ ■

Imagine a two-story house containing about 2,000 square feet of living space. Now, in your mind, choose any architectural style for the house, and picture it on an open piece of land of about half an acre. Now place that house and land in various locations and consider its relative value: Located on oceanfront property the value is very high; set in a suburban middle-class neighborhood the value is also modified by the location; placed in a rural environment

with a beautiful view of the mountains or rolling plains, the value would be affected by the quality of that view. Although the specific values can be widely divergent across the United States, a house in the suburban middle-class neighborhood worth $100,000 could be worth 10 times that amount on the ocean and 3–5 times that amount in a location with good mountain views.

■ ■ ■

The visual aesthetics of a site — whether it be an ocean setting, a view of the mountains, or a wide panorama of the plains — are the primary factors determining the value of a particular house built there. The factor of commuting distance does affect the perceived value of a residential location; however, when given two locations within the same commuting distance, the one with the better site aesthetics will have a higher selling price. (This is not true for a business site, since proximity to a customer base or particular supplier may have a greater influence in adding value.)

According to the book *Value by Design* by the Urban Land Institute, most home buyers think

Location plays a very important role in determining the value of property. A particular house located in a suburban neighborhood (A) would have a much higher value if it was placed on oceanfront property (B), and yet another value if situated in a rural setting with a mountain view (C).

that if the landscaping of the entire community is of a high quality, they will get a good return on the money they invest in a house in that neighborhood.

Realtors are able to establish and quantify the relative value added by a good location by reviewing home property values in a given location over time. Until recently, however, it has been difficult to quantify the value that good landscaping adds to a particular property. In essence, assessing the value added by landscaping refines the concept of a given location to include not only where the property is and what the surrounding area is like, but also the "personal" characteristics of the property itself — that is, the landscaping.

Quantifying the Value of Landscaping

Just as the perceived value of property fluctuates according to popular attitudes and perceptions about how much something is worth, so do the perceived values of good landscaping fluctuate.

How Value Is Determined

When economists set out to determine the value of something, they draw on a concept known as "willingness to pay." The principle is that the value of an object or service is demonstrated every time someone buys it. Producers of goods and services sometimes refer to this concept as "whatever the market will bear." In other words, a value is determined to a great extent by what the consumers feel it is worth. The more people who believe it, the stronger the validation that the price is worth it. If more people want it and it is not available, the price goes even higher.

Monetary valuation of landscapes, or of any other environmental benefits for that matter, is not something most economists are willing to recognize. Instead of assessing a specific monetary value for a landscape, an economist will do what is called a "cost/benefit analysis" — the determination of a value (or of an increase in value) depends on proving that the benefit derived from the goods or services exceeds the cost of creating it. An increase in the quality of life is certainly a benefit, but it is so subjective that it is difficult to quantify in monetary terms.

Landscaping is one of these fairly subjective benefits that are difficult to quantify. Real estate agents may have an idea of how much a home with a great landscape is worth but, as the *Portland Press Herald* real estate columnist Edith Lank says, "Buyers make value. That's the appraiser's axiom, and it's absolutely true. It doesn't matter what real estate agents think your house is worth, or what you think it's worth. . . . The one thing that counts is the judgment of the buying public."

How Landscaping Value Is Assessed

Traditionally the house structure and its property are valued separately. In the United States, we are accustomed to the separate values for structure and property assigned for tax purposes. The landscape or "yard" actually connects these two entities and makes them one. Home buyers think of themselves as buying the entire package and not component parts. How effectively you have created this connection in large part determines what type of return you

While good landscaping alone doesn't hold much value from a tax standpoint, it can greatly increase the value of an otherwise unimpressive house. An effective landscape makes the house and yard appear as a single, impressive entity.

will get. Bear this in mind as you consider your investment; it presents one of the primary arguments for drawing on the services of a qualified landscape design professional in planning how to invest your money.

As far as property taxes are concerned, plantings usually are not considered a taxable improvement, unlike physical improvements or construction additions to the property. As plantings mature, they increase not only in inherent value but also in the value they add by making your home a nicer place to live. Plants add this value without associated property tax increases.

How Homeowners Perceive Landscaping Values

As we've mentioned, if enough people believe something is very valuable, it becomes so. According to the many Realtors with whom this was discussed, prior to the 1980s less than 15 percent of people purchasing homes considered the landscape to be of any benefit. Today, there is evidence that a growing number of homeowners believe that landscaping contributes to an increased resale value of a home. In 1993, according to a Gallup poll, more than 35 percent of the public felt that well-maintained landscaping had an impact in the increase of a home's real estate value. In 1994, the percentage had increased to close to 50 percent.

The aesthetics of a homesite appeal strongly to the emotions. People essentially confirm what aesthetic effects are important to them by spending their money on them. The examples of the housing developments of 7979 Westheimer in Houston and the Woodlands in Minneapolis/Saint Paul (see box) point up the appeal of open space and landscapes to both individuals and communities. People's willingness to pay more money for something emotionally appealing is positive proof that an aesthetic approach can be formed that appeals to a large group of people and not just one person's sense of beauty.

EXAMPLES OF VALUE-ADDING LANDSCAPE

The Urban Land Institute's study *Value by Design* reports two examples of the positive economics of having good landscaping on a property.

In Houston, Texas, the renovation of a multi-family garden apartment complex built in 1972 (known as 7979 Westheimer) brought a significant turnaround in the value of the property. Before the renovation project, the complex was vacant and had fallen into disrepair. As part of the seven-month renovation project, the number of apartment units was decreased from 484 to 459 and parking spaces from 914 to 680, thus reducing the project's density. A lush, semi-tropical landscape was established. With this increase in open space, the apartments were transformed from an eyesore to an attractive and successful multi-family community. As a result of the improved appearance and the owner's committment to maintenance, rents in the complex are about 15 percent higher than its closest competition, and the average occupancy level of 96 percent beats competitors by about 12 percentage points.

Another success story is the Woodlands, a housing development on a 72-acre, partially wooded site outside the Twin Cities of Minneapolis/Saint Paul. Careful attention to site planning, preservation of natural resources, and landscape design in the building of this project helped it to achieve a strong identity and market acceptance. The value that residents receive from the landscape and amenities as quality of life and financial investment is perceived as a high premium. Values of new houses have increased — as the community developed and neared its goal of 122 dwellings, the value of the houses grew.

Money Spent on Landscaping

In 1994, the baby boomer population alone spent $6.2 billion on professional "green-industry services" such as lawn care, tree care, nursery products, and landscape construction. Consumer spending for professional landscape design services almost doubled between 1993 and 1994, rising from $488 million to $869 million. This increase reflects the addition of 300,000 more households purchasing landscape design services. The projections for 1995 are an increase of 1.1 million more households. This is almost a fourfold increase (Gallup Survey results comparing 1993 to 1994). A study by the "Home Enthusiast Panel" of *Better Homes and Gardens* found that landscaping rated #1 on Americans' lists of planned home improvement projects. One out of three of the respondents said they plan to build a deck or patio.

Are There Standards for Evaluating Aesthetics?

While beauty is in the eye of the beholder and can be very subjective, there are, however, general features that a majority of people find attractive or appealing. By designing and building to meet those criteria you can increase the likelihood that most people will find a given space attractive.

It is not enough to say that a landscaped yard is likely to be more valuable than one that is not landscaped; the aesthetic quality of the landscaping is also a factor. Imagine three identical

---

MITIGATING FACTORS YOU MAY NOT BE ABLE TO CHANGE

As you analyze the value that may be added to your property by an aesthetically pleasing landscape, you should keep in mind any mitigating factors that may outweigh these benefits. These are factors that, in a cost/benefit analysis (see page 12), may make the cost of installing the landscaping exceed the benefits gained. They include:

- The general condition of the neighborhood
- The location of the neighborhood itself
- The current value of the house before landscaping

In most cases, it will be difficult to raise the value of a given piece of property much above the highest property value in that neighborhood. If the neighborhood has generally low property values, you should think carefully about how much you want to invest in your landscape and how high you can raise your property value. If you "overlandscape" for the neighborhood you may not be able to recoup your initial investment. An extreme example would be if you were to build a beautiful Japanese garden in a run-down neighborhood. Although the Japanese garden adds value to the neighborhood, the neighborhood decreases the potential value of the garden. However, for the investor who is willing to take a risk, this principle of the locality directing the general value of property can actually work to your benefit: If, over time, the entire neighborhood's appearance is improved through good landscaping, all of the property values can go up significantly.

You also should consider the current value of the house and land without landscaping: If a house is in relatively poor shape and has little to offer a prospective buyer in terms of function or location, you could create the most beautiful landscape in the world and not increase the salability of the lot. Beauty goes hand in hand with other attributes that need to be considered in assessing value based on aesthetics.

houses in the same neighborhood — one beautifully landscaped, one not landscaped at all, and the third weed infested, with overgrown shrubs blocking the view of the house. It is fairly obvious that there would be different asking prices for the homes where all else was equal.

To help you better understand the contribution that aesthetics make to the value of a home, we have provided a model for aesthetic evaluation in the form of a tally sheet that offers you an opportunity to determine how your own landscape ranks. This is found in Appendix 1 on page 148. After using this audit to evaluate your own landscape and grounds, you will have a good idea of what needs to be done to maximize the value of your property through design improvements. It will also prioritize the actions and steps to be taken. Remember, although beauty is in the eye of the beholder, the tally sheet will lead to a landscape that holds the greatest appeal to the largest number of people.

3

How Much Are Trees and Other Landscaping Elements Worth?

WE ALL KNOW THAT TREES AND OTHER plantings have some intrinsic value. The difficulty lies in quantifying that value. There are many factors that influence the value of a tree or, in certain circumstances, a landscape. While some of these factors are unique to a particular tree or are determined by conditions other than its actual physical characteristics (as we will discuss later in this chapter), the tree itself is a good place to begin.

Important Factors Influencing Tree Value

As you set out to evaluate the value of a particular tree on your property or a piece of property you are considering buying, there are some primary factors to consider, such as the type of

tree, condition, location, and the functions the tree serves. These factors have a direct influence on the value of the tree. For instance, a tree with poor roots will be devalued accordingly. Likewise, location conditions such as proximity to a hazardous site will reduce the tree's value. A tree planted directly beneath a power line will be less valuable than the exact same tree planted in an open yard.

By considering these factors, we can evaluate individual trees objectively.

Other Factors Influencing Value

To refine our understanding of the concept of worth a bit more, think of an object such as a huge old teakettle. To determine the value of the kettle, you need to know if you are making an estimate of the cost of replacing it if it becomes broken or for insurance purposes in case it is stolen. That is, are you determining the cost of buying a new one that looks like the old, or the cost of acquiring one that has exactly the same value as the original? While you may be able to buy a new kettle that looks like the old one for $XX, the old one may have some extra value added by "pre-existing conditions." For instance, is it an antique? Was it made by Paul Revere? Was it once owned by a famous person who scratched his name into it? Factors such as these can increase value significantly. In the case of trees and landscape plantings, a num-

ber of different factors can affect the assessed value of trees depending on the planned use for the tree and its placement in the landscape.

How Context Influences Tree Value

As you identify the factors that are relevant to assessing the value of a specific tree, you may discover that the particular context you're working within affects the value factors. For instance, let's say a 40-inch-diameter black walnut tree, with a straight trunk and no branches until it is

---

PRIMARY FACTORS INFLUENCING TREE VALUE

Size
- Diameter
- Height
- Spread

Number of trunks
- Single stem
- Multistem

Site
- Residential: urban, suburban
- Commercial
- Collegiate
- Rural: forest, field, swamp

Location
- Aesthetic enhancement (framing/depth)
- Proximity to utility lines and/or structures

Stand density
- Single tree
- Light
- Moderate
- Heavy

Species
- Regional appropriateness
- Degree of maintenance required
- Uniqueness or rarity
- Susceptibility to diseases or insect infestations

Method of Valuation Influence (24-inch black walnut veneer value vs. aesthetic contribution)

Condition
- Crown/leaves
- Roots
- Trunk
- Branching
- General vigor
- Hazardous

Placement (appropriateness for function)

Function of tree
- Screening
- Shade
- Financial contribution
- Recreation
- Framing
- Wind buffer

History
- Specific historical interest
- Costs of past treatments
- Impact on income (direct or indirect, due to increased costs of heating and cooling)

Emotional (sentimental or romantic attachment)

---

32 feet off the ground, is growing in your front yard. Although the shade provided by the tree is important to you, this value will most likely be outweighed by what you will gain selling it to a veneer mill. The veneer mill's price will be based on market demand for black walnut veneer.

The other trees on your property can also affect the process used to assess value of a particular tree. For example, if you live on a wooded lot, each individual tree does not carry the same value as a tree of the same species that is well placed on the lot. Each tree could have exactly the same diameter, same general health and vigor, and be in roughly the same place, but the wooded lot means that the tree is not unique and therefore doesn't contribute equally to the site.

Placing value on a tree becomes particularly subjective when you rely on emotional factors. How do you put a dollar value on an object that means a lot to you personally but may not mean anything to someone else? For example, consider the black walnut tree discussed previously. Imagine that your grandfather planted that tree in honor of his father — you wouldn't sell it for even twice the veneer value because it would dishonor your grandfather and great-grandfather.

Determining the Cost of Replacing the Tree

One of the simplest ways to place a value on a tree or plant is to calculate how much it would cost to replace it with a plant of comparable type, size, and appearance. This method of valuation can show a significant return on your investment because, unlike most objects you buy, plants tend to appreciate in value rather than depreciate since they grow and improve with age. For example, say you bought some 15- to 18-inch spreading yews at $20 each and planted them as an evergreen hedge. Within ten years, the plants will have grown to a size of three feet tall and four feet wide and have a value of $60 each. They will triple in replacement value over time with only minimal maintenance on your part. The same amount of money in, say, a certificate of deposit that returned 10 percent after taxes (good luck!) would make only $27.16 on each $20 invested.

Determining replacement value, however, is not as straightforward as it at first seems. Consider the following points:

- **What constitutes cost?** Is it the wholesale cost of the plant or the retail cost? Is it the cost of the plant plus the cost of labor for professionally installing it? Should you include the cost of the

---

HOW MUCH IS A TREE WORTH?

There are a number of methods for determining how much a tree is worth — some that are straightforward and objective and others that are more subjective. These methods include:

- Cost of replacing the tree (as determined by size)
- Extrapolated value per square inch based on cost of replacement (according to Trunk Formula Method of the Council of Tree and Landscape Appraisers)
- Cost of treatment for disease or maintenance problems
- Value of environmental contributions of tree
- Value of tree as pulpwood
- Value of veneer from tree
- Value of tree as sawlog
- Historical value
- Aesthetic contribution to landscape
- Value of tree as it affects income
- Emotional value

amendments used when planting? What about the cost of specialized equipment that may be necessary to plant it?

- ■ **Is it reasonable to replace the plant?** Once plants get beyond a certain size, it becomes unrealistic to attempt a replacement. A replacement for a tree more than six inches in diameter at breast height is very difficult to find at a nursery. You may be able to find a tree growing in the wild (maybe your own backyard) but you need to consider the massive amount of time and effort that would go into attempting such a replacement.

- ■ **Is this a common plant in the trade?** If your plant is very rare in the nursery trade, what is the likelihood that you can find a replacement the same size as the one you've grown, not to mention the same condition?

Calculating Tree Replacement Value by Formula

A tree that has grown beyond the size that can be replaced easily is commonly evaluated by the Trunk Formula Method established by the CTLA (Council of Tree and Landscape Appraisers). This valuation method is administered by the International Society of Arboriculture and is used by professional consulting arborists across the United States. It is based upon the replacement value of that tree per square inch and extrapolated to the number of square inches on the surface of the plane of the trunk of the tree (imagine the top of a stump). Once this base value is determined for the tree, several factors are considered that could affect that value: species, condition, location.

This method of valuation is often used for insurance purposes as well as in court cases where an offending party (usually a neighbor) has cut, poisoned, or removed trees on a person's property. It can be quite a challenge at times

to determine the general condition of a tree that is no longer there, let alone determine the type of tree it was. It can take some real detective work on the part of the arborist, but it is not impossible.

Replacement cost is determined by consensus within a state or a region — there are too many variables to apply this nationwide. Once the replacement value per square inch is established, the arborist measures the tree's dbh (diameter at breast height — about 4 feet off the ground), identifies the species of tree, determines its general condition, and considers not only the implications of the site on the tree but also the effect of the tree on the site. All of that information is rolled into a complete formula. This is too complicated for the average homeowner to calculate, but an arborist can do it for you.

Cost of Treatments or Repairs

Another method of calculating the value of a tree or plant is to add up the ongoing costs of maintaining and caring for the tree or a landscape. If you have been outlaying a certain amount of money each year for fertilizers and mulch for your shrub bed, this is an investment that you have made annually to maintain a certain level of general appearance. If the shrubs were azaleas and they suffered an attack of azalea sawfly, you may have bought an insecticide or paid a professional maintenance company to control these pests. The money you have spent was used to enhance the inherent aesthetic value of the landscape. It is an expenditure that you can record and substantiate.

Natural disasters may also be a factor to consider in calculating repair and maintenance costs. If the landscape was destroyed because of flood or hurricane damage, what would it take to recreate a reasonable facsimile of it in its previous condition? This can be a significant sum of money depending on the maturity of the landscape. In order to seek this kind of value — say for insurance purposes — it is essential that pre-existing conditions be faithfully recorded and updated. Photographs and plant measurements should be tracked at least yearly. The original cost of the plants as well as subsequent maintenance treatments or repairs need to be noted. This method of assessing value is most significant for landscapes that are officially "recognized" in some way, such as valuable public sites or award-winning gardens. However, we feel that the homeowner should also keep an up-to-date inventory of property and landscape in case of natural disaster.

The Value of Environmental Contributions

Trees and other landscape plantings make significant contributions to our general health and well-being. This happens not only globally and regionally, but also privately and individually. The United States Forest Service recently conducted a three-year study in the downtown Chicago area. It was trying to quantify the positive effects that trees offer in general and comparing that to the costs of maintaining those trees over a given period of time. The study demonstrated that the planting of 95,000 trees in a selected area would benefit the communities as much as $38 million over a period of about thirty years. This is above and beyond the costs associated with maintaining those trees. The trees studied were green ash, which has relatively high maintenance needs. They were chosen because they were typical of trees found in the Chicago study area. If a lower-maintenance tree were to be used and the planting environment were to be improved to better meet the tree's cultural requirements, the return could go up significantly.

Air Quality

One of the most important contributions that leafy plants provide is the exchange of carbon dioxide into oxygen. Since carbon dioxide is a waste product of our breathing and we have a need for a certain amount of oxygen in our atmosphere to breathe, this is a very important contribution. Because of the vast size of this green gas exchanger, the value of a single plant or even a group of plants is relatively insignificant in this regard. When considered en masse, or globally, however, this commodity's price would be impossible to affix because of its value to the existence of life itself.

Weather Patterns

Another massive contribution provided by plants is their effect on regional weather patterns. Because of the transfer of moisture into the air and the effect of radiational cooling, plants influence weather locally and also in remote areas of the globe. This is a value that also eludes any individual analysis because the basis for it is realized only in the large scale.

Pollution Control

One global environmental contribution provided by plantings is as a filter of pollution. A single three-inch-diameter tree can annually filter out the pollution of a single automobile driven ten miles by removing the carbon that it has emitted. Again, this is a value that is difficult to apply to a single plant or even a landscape grouping because of the sheer volume of other plants that also function in this capacity. It can be quantified, however, over a large enough area. In the Chicago study, it was found that for a two-county area, polluting agents such as ozone, carbon monoxide, and sulfur dioxide were removed — at a value of more than $9 million.

In choosing the best plants for pollution removal, you need to consider the leaf mass of the trees and shrubs. A plant with relatively small leaves and little crown density is not as effective as a tree with a larger leaf and high crown density. For example, in the Chicago study, it was discovered that buckthorn made up close to 13 percent of the total number of trees but it represented a little less than 3 percent of the leaf surface of all of the trees. Replacing these plants with leafier and more effective pollution-filtering trees would significantly increase those benefits.

Energy Consumption Reduction

The specific environmental contributions made by plants that are quantifiable are those that influence the cost of operating the heating and cooling systems for a building. In these cases, mature trees are known as a value-adding commodity. Their loss would result in an immediate and measurable increase in the operating utility costs of the building. A properly placed deciduous tree will reduce heat buildup in a building during hot summer days, and in the winter, when the leaves are gone, it allows light through to supplement heating efforts. A row of evergreens planted in just the right location acts as a wind buffer in the winter and can reduce heat loss resulting from the buffeting winds.

How can you plant to take advantage of the plants' potential? It is largely dependent on where you live or work. The strategic placement of these plants is determined by the angle of the sun from winter through summer and back again to winter. A tree in the United States is probably best planted on the west side of a house to provide the maximum shade and protection. Prevailing winds are primarily from the west and the heat of the day builds up there so it is far more effective than planting on the east side. Planting on the east side creates shade in the morning that blocks the sun's warmth when you want to take advantage of it. Remember, though, the best planting scheme depends on the direction of the prevailing winds in your own community. A qualified landscape professional in your community can offer the best advice, since there is a good deal to know about the most effective plantings for energy cost reductions. For example, even the species of trees (which also is influenced by where you live) can have a big impact on the efficacy of the plantings. The density of the branching structure of a maple is far less than that of a Kentucky coffee tree. A greater density of branching will also cause a greater reduction in available sunlight during the winter — therefore, you would not get the best return on your landscape dollar. Another factor to consider in the choice of a tree is how early the leaves drop from the tree in the fall and how late they arrive in the spring. (The catalpa is a tree that is exemplary in this regard, as are many ash trees.)

Microclimates

One other way in which plantings can promote an environmental value is by developing microclimates on your property. A tree can create a shady area that will in turn create a breeze because of the temperature differential between the hot air outside the tree canopy and the cooler air under the crown of the tree. Plants can also act as mechanisms to divert cold air or to contain warm air. Marginally hardy plants can be given a greater security of survival from these influences.

Wildlife and Ecology

A dead tree can still contribute in a positive way from an environmental perspective. Sometimes referred to as "habitat" trees, dead trees perform a vital ecological function by being an abode for agents of decay as well as homes for other forest- or field-dwelling critters. These animals in turn act as a food source for other animals. The process of decay also redistributes assets that have already been depleted from the forest floor. Imagine the condition of the soil in any forest after decades of continual harvesting and removal of trees. It is highly unlikely that any artificial soil additive could replace what trees would have provided. En masse these trees are essential and hold great value, but it is difficult, if not impossible, to assign a specific monetary value to any individual habitat tree.

The Value of a Tree for Pulpwood, Veneer, and Sawlogs

In some parts of the country and from one perspective the greatest value of a tree is based on its use in the paper or lumber industries. Pulpwood is used for manufacturing papers and other paper-related products such as cardboard boxes. Generally the relatively soft and fibrous woods, such as pines, are used for this purpose.

Veneer is wood that is processed by being peeled from a log in a thin strip. This is adhered to the surface of a cheaper wood or particleboard or other similar surface to convey the illusion that the whole piece is a solid piece of wood that is of the same type as the veneer. Typical trees used in this process are walnut, cherry, oak, and teak.

Sawlogs are used for producing lumber for manufacturing buildings and other structures. Pine, spruce, fir, hemlock, maple, oak, and ash are commonly seen at sawmills.

Trees are also used for specialty purposes. For example, American basswood is prized by wood-carvers because it is lightweight and resists splitting. White ash is used for making baseball bats. Walnut and cherry are used by cabinetmakers for manufacturing fine furniture.

Ebony is used for piano keys, tuning pegs on stringed instruments, and other esoteric applications. Oak is often used in the construction of furniture and hardwood flooring. Some real treasures are sometimes hidden on a piece of land. Remember, one person's firewood is another person's treasure — something that person is willing to pay handsomely for.

Historic or Heritage Value

Sometimes a single plant will have an extremely high value because of some historical or other significant event associated with it. When this happens, a number of factors will influence the specific value. Obviously the loss of this type of a tree will affect not only the site where it was growing but also the economics and possibly the social fabric of the community. A good example of this is the "Treaty Oak" in Texas. Someone had poisoned the tree's roots and surrounding ground with a powerful undiluted herbicide. This caused enormous concern for the city. A historic landmark was threatened, as were tourist dollars and all of the economic spin-offs related to that income. There was an outpouring of support from all over the country. Experts were consulted and preventive and corrective action was undertaken. What is the value of that tree? It isn't measured in board feet or pulpwood, and it isn't derived from the aesthetic values it might offer or the replacement value per square inch. Some would contend that its value can't be measured, it is that great. The value of the tree itself can be approximated, but revenue lost to the community and the investments in maintaining the tree must also be considered.

Another example, from Kiev in Ukraine, demonstrates that this type of value is not limited to the United States. The "Zaporizhia Oak" was Ukraine's most famous tree. Thousands of tourists from all over the world visited this 700-year-old, 118-foot landmark that at one time cast its shadow on Cossack settlements and medieval princes signing treaties and other documents. During the 1970s, a drainage system was built to protect the tree from flooding caused by nearby reservoirs. Ironically, when the drainage system broke in 1994, it went unrepaired. By the time experts were called in from the former Soviet Union and Eastern Europe, it was too late. To add insult to injury, imagine the great cost associated simply with removing a 118-foot-tall tree. The loss of the tourist income affected the local economy and the community's cultural heritage and overall identity. It is easy to measure the economic impact, but it is impossible to measure the other losses associated with the death of this tree. In many respects, it is these other losses which are the greatest and most costly.

Aesthetic Value

Beauty is in the eye of the beholder and as such it can be very difficult to define. Personal taste, family roots, and regional and cultural influences (as well as degrees of exposure to light and shade) can influence an individual's sense of aesthetics. This area of value is difficult, but not impossible, to quantify. The math becomes tricky because of the mitigating factors related to it in the real world, but it can be measured. One of the problems in measuring beauty is that an aesthetic quality can impart a negative influence on value instead of a positive one. This means that you need to find a way of defining *unattractive* in addition to defining *beautiful*.

Effect on Income

It is possible that the loss of a tree or portions of your landscape can affect your income directly. Looking at what would be lost if the

plantings were gone is another way of determining and placing value. To best understand this, look back at some of the environmental contributions already mentioned. What are the extra costs that result from the loss of a tree or shrubs that shaded a house in the summer in a hot climate? How much extra drain on income would result from a loss of a portion of a windbreak that protected a house from heat-stealing wind in a cold northern climate?

Because the cause and effect is subtle, the connection between tree loss and expendable income is rarely seen. There often is no reaction if the loss of a planting of this type occurs. Unless the homeowner analyzes the utility costs of a building both before and after a tree loss, the difference generally goes unnoticed.

When a home or, for that matter, any building is sold, are the energy savings provided by the landscape considered in calculating the value of that property? If the energy savings are $50 a month, that is $600 a year or $6,000 in ten years or $60,000 in one hundred years. To get an even better understanding of the economic impact, imagine that you are a new homeowner and you are 25 years old. You are going to live in the house for 40 years. If you were to take the money you saved each month and put it into a mutual fund that returned 10 percent per annum after taxes, at the end of 40 years you would have $108,566 — with an outlay of only $24,000!

Emotional Value

The Lorax of Dr. Seuss fame said, "I speak for the trees for they have no tongues." That character embodied the spirit of many people around the world. Lovers of nature and things that grow have a strong emotional attachment to trees. Another often-heard line is "Woodsman, spare that tree!" In our many years of being in this business, we've lost track of the number of heated discussions in a person's yard over the value of keeping a single tree — even when there is too much competition from other trees for any of them to grow well. Even when that single tree is almost dead. Even when that same single tree is producing a hazardous situation for the person arguing to spare it.

Emotions cannot be denied. They can be strongly associated with a value system or cultural pride. Strong emotions can be rooted in memories, without logic or explanation. It has also been said that "everyone has his price." This is where the assessment of a reasonable price can be difficult if not impossible. You may be willing to sacrifice your emotional attachment for a huge sum of money, but it is unlikely that anyone who is not sympathetic to your emotions will pay it.

Using the Advice of Professionals

All the ways a tree or a landscape can be valued are based on the circumstances surrounding it. If you are taking a case to court, for example, we recommend retaining the services of a professional arborist with extensive knowledge about the valuation of trees. This knowledge is essential for an equitable assessment of the dollar value. In court, the arborist will be acting on your behalf. He or she will be able to demonstrate why the tree is being evaluated as it is. The arborist may inform you that the tree has little value under the current circumstances and that you should not pursue the issue. It is always recommended that you get a second opinion, but be careful that you are not just looking for someone to tell you what you want to hear.

4

Landscaping Considerations When Building, Buying, or Selling a House

~

WHETHER YOU ARE BUILDING, BUYING, or selling a home, the land and landscape have an inherent value. By recognizing that the landscape is valuable, you can take full advantage of its potential. You are less likely to waste money and more likely to see and then seize the opportunities for adding money to your pocket. If you are building a house, you may be saving yourself thousands of dollars in future expenses if you protect and preserve the right trees. If you are buying a house, you may be adding just the right plants in just the right place and you will be enhancing the livability of the space and therefore adding value to the quality of your life. When you put that house on the market, the trees and plants will have matured and will add significantly to the home's emotional appeal to prospective buyers.

Building a House

If you're thinking of building a home, many other important things should be considered. Assume for this portion of the chapter that you have already purchased a piece of land. The size of the lot will alter some of the points here, but for the most part these suggestions hold true for lots of all sizes.

There are many important reasons you should include the landscape contractor, designer, or architect in the building process right from the beginning. The first and perhaps most important function these professionals can perform is to help you preserve valuable landscape features already on the lot. This can be of value to you immediately, as well as later on if you decide to sell. The Urban Land Institute's book *Value by Design* describes how residents in a number of communities from all over the United States stated that "passive amenities" such as views, open spaces, and trees were important in their decision to purchase. A professional can help you to identify any valuable trees, to determine the best placement of the house, to set a realistic budget, and to outline a design and construction schedule.

Assessing Existing Trees

When you are looking at the trees on the property where you are building, you will first want to identify what types of trees they are. Certain types of trees can be more beneficial to the yard than others. For example, a sugar maple may be just the right shade tree for your front yard. It provides four-season interest, from tapping for syrup in the spring and luxuriant shade in the summer, to orange to yellow fall color and a stately form in the winter. It is also a long-lived tree, lasting for generations. In fact, on some old farms established in the 1800s, it was not uncommon for families to plant maples in a grove form, with each tree representing a member of the family. Many of these groves can still be found to this day. An example of a commonly planted tree that is not as desirable is the poplar. The poplar, which is short lived, has a bland yellow fall color and is very susceptible to blowover and storm damage — not a very valuable tree. Given a choice between the two, it would be more likely that you would try to save the maple than the poplar.

This is looking at only practical and aesthetic considerations. If you looked at the value of the trees according to the Council of Tree and Landscape Appraisers (CTLA) method (8th edition), you would find that there is a significant difference in monetary value between a twelve-inch-diameter sugar maple and a twelve-inch-diameter poplar. All things being equal, and if they were in comparable positions in the landscape and were contributing the same to the site, the maple would be valued at $3,200 and the poplar at only $1,200. There are, however, exceptions to every rule. Two exceptions that may arise in this case are if the maple tree is in a poor location and if it is a hazardous tree — that is, if it has structural problems, such as a hollow center, rotten or dead limbs, brittle branches, leaning, or an unbalanced crown, and may harm property or people. If you are not familiar with the different types of trees, how would you know? It is unlikely that you would know unless you had studied arboriculture or had field experience. This is why it is important to use

Sugar Maple Tree

Poplar Tree

Some trees are more valuable than others. For example, a sugar maple tree is long lived and offers shade, color, and an attractive shape, while a poplar is short lived, has bland fall color, and is subject to storm damage. These are facts to consider when deciding what trees to keep on your property.

the services of a professional arborist or other landscape professional.

Trees are so valuable that you should use several techniques to protect them. First, make sure there is a tree-protection clause in your contract or contract specifications with the builder. This should include a statement assessing accountability of damage (including problems that arise later) to the contractor. Consult with a professional arborist in the writing of this portion of the specifications or contract. One method that helps is to have a money value placed on the trees (see chapter 3) and make signs stating their value. Place these signs prominently on the trees. In this way, if an unknowing tradesman starts to dump something such as concrete on the roots, he will be reminded that he wouldn't want to have to pay the replacement cost. Storm fencing can also be used to keep people and equipment away from the ever-important root system. These fences should be placed at least as far out as around the tree's drip edge (the outer tree leaf area). You may want to set out

When building a house, be sure to protect the trees you want to save by letting construction workers know just how valuable they are (with a sign) and encircling them with storm fencing.

stakes along the drip edge and use fluorescent surveyor's tape to cordon that area off in order to protect the root zone from compaction. The bright colors of these tapes serve as a constant reminder of how important you feel the trees are.

When you are having trees removed, make sure that the trees that are cut are not of lumber quality. You certainly don't want to turn good timber into firewood or pulp when part or most of the lumber you need for building your house is right on your land. A word to the wise: If someone offers to remove the trees for you at a price that seems too good to be true, it is likely that he or she may be selling the tree for its lumber value. If you have a large wooded lot, you may want to have the entire piece of property looked at for timber harvesting. This should be done with the help of your state's forestry service. The correct management of a woodlot could be a moneymaker for you. It can also provide firewood, wildlife habitat, and a place for recreation for your whole family. Cross-country-ski and nature trails are just two ideas for a sizable tract of land.

Adding or Clearing Trees

If you live in an area with no or few trees, you will want to talk to someone about the types of trees you can plant. These could be ornamental trees, forest canopy trees, or even production-oriented plantings. Examples of production plantations are pine for lumber or paper production, balsam fir for Christmas trees or nursery sales, or an apple orchard. An orchard can be a source for the home fruit-grower to produce not only apples, but also cider, jellies, and even wines or vinegars. In some states, tree plantations or woodlots can mean certain tax advantages. When these lots are managed and harvested regularly, the property owner may get property tax relief. One caveat — if you sell the property as house lots in the future, you will be responsible for the unpaid tax difference. The state wants to have the land kept in trees; if you cease to grow the trees and change the use, you will be penalized.

If you are building in a dense grove of trees, you need to be aware that you could be creating a dangerous situation. The construction of the building requires that you create an opening in the middle of this grove. The problem is that the trees along this new perimeter will be very likely to uproot in moderate to heavy winds. Evergreen trees are generally far more prone to this problem. This is exacerbated even more if the trees were manually planted in rows. Whenever you plan on building within or on the edges of woods, it is particularly important that you consult first with a knowledgeable and experienced forester or arborist.

Selecting House Location

Once you have located the important trees, you will then want to look at the location of the house. First, consider the boundary setbacks as required by the town you live in.

For many reasons, the lay of the land is extremely important in determining proper house location. For instance, don't locate your future home in a low, wet area, which may indicate a spring. Springs can be permanent and run all year, or may have a seasonal flow that fluctuates according to the amount of rainfall in the vicinity. Knowing that it exists can help you change it from a liability to a possible asset. It could be the source for an artificial stream or a future pond. It would not be a good place to have a basement. Another type of wet area you may come across in construction is what is known as a "vernal pool," a temporary wet area that dries up after spring. These are important recharge areas for amphibians such as toads, salamanders, and frogs have recently been added to lists of protected areas. Although a vernal pool is not submerged in water all year round, it is still considered a wetland.

If the land you are building on is in a region that is prone to flooding or to major storms such as hurricanes, northeasters, or tropical depressions, you need to consider how the lot's topography will adversely affect any buildings there. In certain situations the land or the existing trees can act as a funnel for wind or water. If you are in one of these paths when a natural disaster occurs, damage is much more likely. Also, structures themselves have an effect on wind patterns. A building's profile could cause snowdrifts in doorways, driving rain coming into your garage, and numerous other problems. By bearing these factors in mind, you will have a greater chance of "weathering the storm."

You will also want to consider the sun and how you can best receive solar gain in northern climates. In the southern United States, cooling in the summer is more important. You need to consider the proximity of the future house to your neighbors, to the road, and to the best views as well. Also consider the impact that the building's profile and footprint will have on sun and shadow locations. This will directly influence plant choices and the design of the landscape.

Depending on the style of architecture you have chosen, the design of the driveway should also be considered. A good rule is to have a turnaround with easy maneuverability. Generally, you don't want to make the drive part of the front yard. Some exceptions to this are sites with insufficient space or that incorporate a courtyard, or where a circular drive lets people off in front of your house. It is usually more desirable to have the drive in a side yard and not the first thing visible in the yard.

If at all possible before you buy land, determine ledge locations. Ledge and groundwater can be mitigating factors that will help in choosing where to locate (or not to locate) your house. Not only can there be great expense from blasting ledge, but it may affect the landscape as well. Future plantings of lawns or trees and shrubs can be severely damaged by rocky outcroppings. Lawns will be more susceptible to drought. Newly planted trees will have less opportunity to set out anchoring roots and will be subject to a greater chance of blowover in high winds. Shrubs and trees both may be more likely to desiccate prematurely. Ledge also can create circumstances of too much water. We were once called to investigate why mature trees on a client's property were mysteriously falling down. There was no apparent cause to this calamity. After questioning the client, we discovered that the most recent activity in the general vicinity of the trees was the construction of a new home. We probed the soil in the area where the trees were growing and discovered a great deal of water. Our probes also revealed that there was ledge several feet below finished grade. Analysis revealed that the new home's foundation had acted as a dam and created an "underground lake" or "perched water table." The ground became too saturated to support the roots and mass of the trees.

Tips for Excavating the Site

When you are excavating the house site, keep one good old Yankee rule in mind: Never throw anything away. In other words, every rock you have dug out of the foundation hole, all the fill, and all the loam should be set aside for reuse. Don't pay to have something removed and then pay again to have it brought back. There are some things, however, that you do want to have removed. During construction, be sure stumps that have been pulled out during site development are taken off-site to an appropriate landfill. Or, if the stumps are to be buried on your building site, be aware that you can expect some slumping to occur. A sinkhole may develop, where the ground completely collapses or opens up. Although this can be a safety concern with small children or pets, the situation is easily remedied by filling. Try to locate a stump dump on your property in an area that is inconspicuous and out of the way. During the construction process, be sure that the contractor maintains a

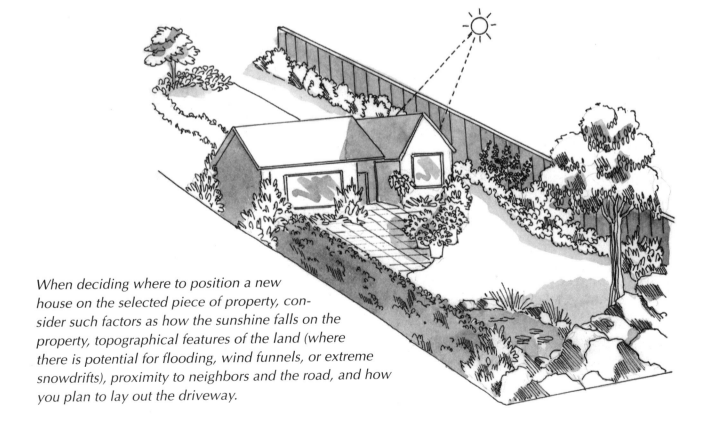

When deciding where to position a new house on the selected piece of property, consider such factors as how the sunshine falls on the property, topographical features of the land (where there is potential for flooding, wind funnels, or extreme snowdrifts), proximity to neighbors and the road, and how you plan to lay out the driveway.

clean and safe work site. One problem that can occur is the indiscriminate dumping and burying of building debris. This can come back to haunt you in later years.

You may also have plants on your site that are worth saving by transplanting them. There are economical and very feasible methods available for transplanting big trees, such as using a tree spade — a hydraulic digging machine shaped like four giant trowels. This method could enable you to save ten- to twelve-foot-tall evergreen trees for a hedge or an apple tree for future fruit and blossoms. Larger trees can be moved by using an excavator and transplanting techniques developed and approved by the American Association of Nurserymen (AAN). A good landscape professional or forester will be able to tell you when it would be cost effective to move plants that are on the site before you start to build.

Another thing to save at the time of site excavation is any soil that has been extracted from the woods. This soil contains a variety of very important elements that may not be present in soil that is brought to the site, such as worms, beneficial insects, and mycorrhiza and other microorganisms that are essential to development of healthy root systems in trees and other woody plants. In addition, there is a vast array

Save the soil excavated from woody areas during home construction to use when you landscape. It is rich in microscopic elements such as worms, beneficial insects, and other nutrient sources for trees and plants.

of other "goodies." Ferns, wildflowers, and other ground covers are there in root form as well as seed or spore. When light, moisture, and air conditions are right, they will spring forth with vigorous new growth. This is especially useful for replenishing the woods margin after the construction disruption. When you are in a large open area such as a field, you should rototill the area and scrape and stockpile the loam, essentially for the same reasons for saving forest humus. Loam set aside from field areas will be valuable for planting trees, shrubs, perennials, and lawns. One caveat — weeds.

A BUILDING BUDGET FOR LANDSCAPING

It is a very good idea to have a landscape budget when you are building your house. Remember that your project will probably cost slightly more than you had planned. Usually new and better ideas will crop up during the construction phase, so be sure to have a realistic budget in mind (see chapter 5). Wouldn't it be great to have some money left over at the end of the project? That is much better than having no money, feeling stressed out, and not enjoying what should be a wonderful experience. After all, in many cases you're building a dream!

Set a budget that will allow you to design your landscape in a way that will complement that dream. Designing the landscape before the construction process is always recommended. If you have to wait to have your "dream" landscape, then do the minimum lawn installation. This stabilizes the soil and you can wait until there are sufficient funds to have the landscape done the way you have designed it. Try not to compromise quality for price. Hold out for that dream landscape. A design is a good idea in any event, because whether you do your yard all at once, or a little each year, you will have a guide to follow and a better idea of the costs you can expect (see chapter 6).

You can reduce the incidence of weed seed in saved loam in several ways. If you have purchased the land and will not be building for a year or two, one way is to mow the field areas before they go to seed. This will give you a hay crop (and positive cash flow). In the northeast United States, fields are mowed twice in a growing season. A second approach to reduce weed seed is to till the area in the spring and overseed with a green manure (buckwheat, winter rye, or clover). This will choke out some of the competing weeds and will add nutrients when you later rototill the loam. Regardless of what approach you take, be sure that the re-spread loam is exposed to the elements for as short a time as possible. The dormant weed seeds will be activated by exposing them to the right conditions for growth. You can also reduce weeds after the loam has been spread for replanting. The first option is to plant the grass immediately to increase the competition with the ever-present weeds. The second option is to let the weeds start to grow after spreading the loam, kill them, and then plant the new lawn.

When putting in a septic system, consider its impact on your future yard and landscape. Make sure you locate the septic field in as inconspicuous a part of the yard as possible. One of the most frequent design problems is trying to hide or camouflage a septic field. This also applies to wells. Consider carefully the location and type of well for your yard. The type of well you choose determines the availability of water and could affect your landscape's general health and vigor. For instance, driven point and dug wells are less expensive but are less reliable in supplying water. Drilled and artesian wells are usually more expensive to have installed, but are generally better and more consistent water suppliers. (See the glossary for more information on wells.) Watering is generally an important contributor to the quality of the landscape. People often consider the importance of water for showers and baths and for washing dishes, clothes, and cars, but overlook the need for adequate water supplies for their landscape. If cost or availability of water is an issue in the area where you plan on building, then you should consider a xeriscape approach to the landscape installation — that is, the use of plants with a high drought tolerance. This will reduce the need for watering.

Buying a House

If you are buying a house with the landscape already inplace, there are many things to consider. Many of these considerations could be helpful as negotiating tools when establishing a purchase price for the home.

Assessing Trees

If you are purchasing a newly built home in a relatively mature stand of trees, be on the lookout for construction damage to those trees. This type of damage is one of the most frequent killers of trees. The death, however, is often not associated with the contractor who did the damage, because of the time lag between the construction and the demise of the tree. You can buy a house on a beautifully treed lot and within several years see every tree die because the building contractor piled fill around the

Before you buy a house, look for signs of possible construction damage to the trees on the property such as crushed roots (left) or fill piled around the base (right).

bases of the trees. This simple act will cause compaction of the soil and will lead to root suffocation. If you purchase a house with trees in this condition, you not only will have a less valuable house, but you also will have expensive tree removals! In addition, this can be dangerous to you and your family. Weakened trees with crushed roots that are slowly suffocating are far more susceptible to wind damage. Many houses and yards are damaged every year by blown-over trees and dead limbs. Anyone who enters your property can be at risk in these situations. (This can also be a lawsuit waiting to happen.) A falling limb has the potential to kill someone! The scary thing about it is that if a limb is ready to fall, it can happen when there is no wind at all. Tree care and knowledge of hazardous trees are obviously very important. A licensed arborist should always be consulted before you buy.

Checking the Quality of the Hardscaping

The quality of the hardscape, the nonliving component of the landscape, is another important factor. For example, a new walkway may look good before winter, but if the base work is not done correctly, then the resulting frost heaving will be dangerous to walk on and expensive to fix. It is therefore important to know how that walk or patio was installed. Stone walls can also be a source of beauty — and danger. A retaining wall that is not correctly constructed with an appropriate batter (a backward and upward slope to the face of the wall) or is without filter fabric may fall over from frost heaving or it may be undermined by water. Correct construction techniques and drainage are essential for a wall's longevity. Where concrete has been used as a retaining wall, check for drainage "weep holes" and inquire about the base. How deep is it? To be completely safe it should be at or below the average frost line. In the northern climates that can be up to four or five feet.

Reviewing the Landscape Layout

When buying a house try to look for a landscape that has been well thought out — a landscape that covers the three basic areas: private, public, and utilitarian (see chapter 6). If you have a trailer or canoe, or if you burn wood for heat, you will want a well-planned area for their storage. Storage areas need to have an easy access to be at their most functional. If you have to go a long way to bring wood in for your stove, you are less likely to use it. It is also important to have ease of access to backyards, oil and gas fills, septic tank covers, and any other utility areas that you are likely to frequent. If these areas are obstructed, it will cost you money to remedy the situation.

Numerous details of the landscape should be considered in the purchase of a structure and property. Is the layout of the lawn and planting beds done in such a way that it makes it difficult to mow? If the yard is small and abutted by neighbors, is privacy available? If the house is in the middle of an open field, is there a windbreak? If you are unfamiliar with plantings in the existing landscape, can the seller provide you with a follow-up care guide for their maintenance?

You can always add to a landscape, so if the things you are looking for are not included you may want to get an idea of what they would cost. By working with a qualified design and construction firm, you could easily attain that information. Armed with this knowledge, you will have a stronger position at the negotiating table.

Selling a House

Selling a house can be difficult for many reasons. Should you sell the house yourself or should you contract with a Realtor? Do you need to make improvements to add to the salability of the home, such as painting, roof repair, or tree pruning? Do you need to do extra maintenance to add to curb appeal? Do you need to plant flowers to add color? Are there sentimental attachments, such as memorial plantings?

Overcoming Emotional Attachments

The first and most important hurdle you have to overcome is your emotional attachment to the house and landscape. Letting go of a home and yard where you have invested thought, time, money, and effort is difficult. "Just as my trees were starting to produce apples I had to leave" is the kind of comment often heard. For those people, planting new trees at their next house may not only be important, it may also be a necessity. Emotional attachment, however, should not get in the way of common sense. Many times people will equate memories and sentimental value with dollar value. It is important to remember that prospective buyers are not likely to be motivated by your emotional attachment, but they will be influenced by overall appearance and neatness of the landscape.

Keeping Up Landscape Maintenance

Small things can make all the difference. First, keeping the lawn mowed and trimmed is essential. Also take time to edge, weed, and prune your shrub and flower beds. Adding mulch will keep the beds' appearance looking better longer, helping with weeds and watering.

Keeping the walks and patios swept and clean is also a good idea. In some cases a coat of water sealant may be just what's needed to give a brick patio a finished and well-kept look. Replacing any cracked or damaged bricks should be done before showing a yard. Make sure any frost heaving has been fixed, although in some less formal types of paths that may not be an issue.

Get your trees pruned, particularly if they have any dead limbs in them. This can be a real deterrent to potential buyers. People want to feel safe in their yard. It is extremely difficult to do that with a big old ugly dead limb hanging overhead.

Adding Color to the Landscape

If you know you are going to be selling next spring — or at some time in the following year — dividing and replanting perennials the fall before is a good idea. Another inexpensive but effective way to dress up the beds is to add drifts of color using bulbs such as tulips, daffodils, grape hyacinths, crocuses, amaryllis, and many other bulbs that might be appropriate for your growing region. Late fall in northern climates is also a good time to fertilize shrubs and trees so that they will have a good start the next spring. This should be done just before the ground freezes or after the plants have lost their leaves.

In the spring, after danger of frost has passed, planting annuals with long blooming cycles in your beds is a nice way to add color inexpensively to your yard. Often, color can attract not only honeybees and hummingbirds, but potential buyers as well. Be sure to deadhead, water, and fertilize your annuals as well as your perennials throughout the summer to keep their appearance up.

Incorporating Good Design Elements

Helping a buyer to feel an emotional connection to the yard can be very powerful. If your yard isn't creating concerns about maintenance, repair, or safety, it will be much easier for individuals to feel comfortable in those surroundings. They will feel more "at home." You want people to appreciate the color, fragrance, and livability that you have had the privilege to experience.

PART II

Where Do I Start?

Developing a Budget and a Plan

5

Budgeting for Landscaping

~

THERE ARE TWO ISSUES TO CONSIDER IN determining how much to budget for landscaping: How much you *can* spend, and how much you *should* spend. The first issue is a rather personal matter which involves reviewing your own financial resources. The second issue — which we will help you determine in this chapter — requires a thorough analysis of your motivations and goals for landscaping, as well as an understanding of what factors are most likely to bring a good return on your investment.

As we discussed in chapters 1 and 2, you can expect a substantial return on your landscaping investment in terms of increasing the resale value of your house. But there are some limiting factors, including the appropriateness of the landscaping to the house, the quality of the landscape design, and the overall property

values of homes in your neighborhood. There are also potential tax benefits to investing your home improvement funds in landscaping, since, for the most part, plantings are not considered a taxable improvement even though they do add value to your property.

Budgeting for the Appropriate Type of Construction

The type of construction project you are contemplating will help determine the budget for landscaping. There are three major categories of construction that involve upgrading landscaping: building a new house, adding on to an existing house, and renovating an older house. Each of these projects involves different landscaping needs and budgets.

Another important factor in determining how much to spend on landscaping is how long and for what purposes you intend to own your home. For instance, do you want to resell it immediately? Within five years? Within twenty years? Or, are you buying this house for your retirement? Your intention to sell or keep a house for a certain period of time is closely related to how much you should and can afford to invest in landscaping — and what kind of landscaping investments are likely to have the greatest returns. Let's take a look at the factors to consider in each of these situations.

Building a New House

If you are planning on building a new house, your major concerns are selecting land, choosing an architect, and picking a builder. Your landscaping will be started from scratch. Before any of these things can happen, you must have financing. (See the section on "How to Finance Landscape Design and Construction" on page 43.)

Building for Immediate Resale

Say you've built a new home valued at $100,000, and you want to sell it immediately. For a good basic landscape, you can expect to invest between ten and fifteen percent of the house's projected value. So in this case, you should budget $10,000 to $15,000 into your construction loan. The reason that you don't invest a smaller amount is that you're less likely to get a major return on your investment.

It's important to emphasize again that this investment assumes a high-quality design and end product. If you just buy $15,000 worth of miscellaneous plants, bricks, stones, and wood, and randomly place them on your property, this won't add any value to your home at all, and may in fact decrease the value.

The plan for the landscaping must go hand in hand with the house-building plan. Select a landscape designer at the same time you select a building contractor. The importance of this connection can't be overstated. Sometimes, simply the position of the house on the property can have a dramatic effect on the entire feeling and character of the home and, if it's successful, can make it more livable. The impact of light, view, air circulation, snow accumulation, and foot and vehicle traffic patterns all must be taken into account when planning where to situate the house. These are the concerns that a good landscape designer will address in the pre-building stage.

Another common problem encountered in new construction is failure to anticipate the effects the contours of the property will have on the house, which can lead to improper drainage, wet basements, water in the garage, and ice buildup near driveways and walks. Once again, a good landscape designer will help you avoid these problems.

MOTIVATIONS FOR OWNING A HOME

There are many different reasons for owning a home. Identifying your own motivation will help you define what kind of landscaping construction and investment makes the most sense and is likely to provide the best return. Here are some of the most common motivations for owning a home. Find the situation that best describes your intention.

- Intend to resell the house immediately
- Intend to resell the house within five to ten years
- Intend to raise a family in the house and resell it in ten to thirty years
- Intend to make the house a permanent residence, dream home, or retirement home

---

Building for Resale in Five to Ten Years

If your plans for reselling your house are longer term, it is important to be aware of your investment goals. Your landscape needs to be mature in order to receive your maximum return on invested dollars. Generally speaking, a landscape takes three to five years to look established. Most trees take much longer. Armed with this information, however, the homeowner can plan a long-term strategy that meets both financial and personal goals.

One example of this strategy would be a plan to install your landscape over a period of six years with a target date of resale in ten years. This approach could make you more money for different reasons. One reason is that you could enter the market with a mature landscape, provided you planned your planting schedule correctly. Another advantage is that rather than borrowing money, you can use discretionary funds to finance your landscape. This optimizes your return with no interest or loan payment obligations. However, there are drawbacks to this approach. The biggest drawback is that you have to wait longer to enjoy the mature landscape. Another obvious problem could arise if the need arose to sell your house on short notice.

If loans are your chosen method of financing the landscape improvements, you should consider rolling your landscape-construction loan in with the loan you took out for building your home. Be sure to make it a separate account that is earmarked specifically for the landscape; otherwise, when cost overruns occur (and they will occur) in the construction of your house, you will be tempted to tap into dedicated landscape reserves.

Building for Resale in Ten to Thirty Years

If you are planning to build a house where you will raise a family, you should consider how children will influence your landscape. They place both financial and functional demands on your yard. A good approach is to spend five to ten percent of the cost of the house on landscaping and then keep a "landscaping reserve fund" to use on landscaping for the special needs of children. For example, they may want a basketball court or an area for volleyball. A common addition to the landscape for children is a swimming pool. This addition must be carefully considered as it rarely returns the money invested. The exception is when the pool area is very carefully planned. All these landscape plans will require money, time, and space. Be sure to plan ahead. Don't make the mistake of spending money on a beautiful shade tree placed next to the pool site. Just as you becoming attached to the tree you may have to cut it down. You will have lost money and something you can never replace — time. Conversely, when your children are leaving home or even just growing out of things in the yard such as sandboxes, you need to consider how those spaces can be converted into usable areas.

Your lifestyle and children may also influence the amount of money you wish to spend on the installation and the continuing maintenance of your yard. Long-term maintenance is a factor that needs to be considered when designing a landscape that is going to give significant return on your investment. If demands on your time, interests, or budget are compromised by a high-maintenance landscape, then you may resent

---

ESTABLISH A SEPARATE ACCOUNT

To make sure that you can accomplish your landscaping goals, we recommend setting aside money for landscaping or yard renovation in a separate bank account. Then make sure that this account isn't used for any other purpose.

---

your yard rather than enjoy it. Financial return will be lessened because of all the associated costs of the years of extensive maintenance. However, if your idea of a good time is mowing, weeding, and general yard care, then disregard the prior statements!

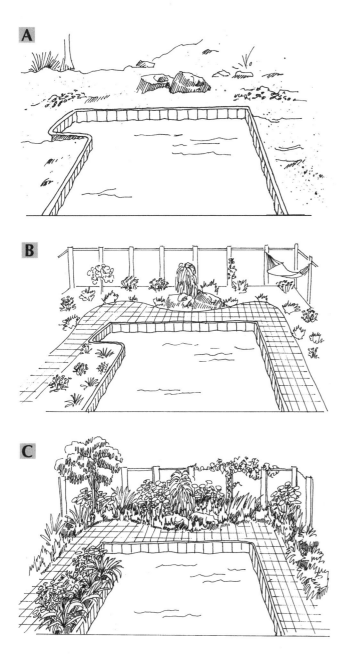

The landscaping for this pool was planned and installed when the pool was built (A), with a vision in mind of what it would look like five years later (B), and ten years later (C), when the owner anticipated he might be ready to sell the property.

Building a Permanent Residence (Retirement or Dream House)

We've all wished and fantasized about the perfect "dream house." "When I win the lottery, I'm going to build this magnificent home!" In most cases, this so-called dream house becomes our permanent home. This notion sometimes becomes a reality. When selecting a site for your dream home, it's important to think about where you're building so that the surrounding homes don't bring your value down. In addition, when you begin the process, we recommend that you closely follow the design procedure outlined in chapter 6. If you choose a landscape designer and contractor for the work, you should still follow our design suggestions.

Once again, financing your dream home is the first step. You should be prepared to spend fifteen to twenty-five percent (or more) of the cost of your home for the landscape. If this is to be your dream house, you may want a swimming pool, a hidden garden, or even an Oriental garden. Whatever your landscape fantasy, those costs should be added to your budget. Your concern here is not for return of money but rather a return of peace of mind and serenity of your surroundings.

We recommend that you interview three landscape firms or architects and choose one you're comfortable with. Cost should not be your only criterion for this selection. How well do the designers/contractors listen to you? Do you feel as though your best interests are being considered? Are they professional? For a complete list of considerations in selecting your contractors, see chapter 10.

When you're past the planning and design phase and into the installation portion of your landscape, you may choose to do this in stages or over a number of years. This depends on your preference, but by doing it all at once you'll enjoy the yard immediately. Or you can save money by taking the longer approach.

These types of homes are not usually thought of as investments or as doubling your return, but if you choose to refinance your home or seek a reverse mortgage to access your equity, or if you need to sell for whatever reason, it's comforting to know that your investment is growing out in your yard.

Adding On to an Existing House

You may need to expand your house because of a new addition to the family, the desire or need for more living space, or the desire to make your house more attractive to sell. Whatever the reason, the budgeting procedure and guidelines are very similar to those recommended for building a new house.

Adding On for Immediate Resale

Let's say you have a home valued at $100,000, and you want to make an addition costing about $20,000. There are several issues to consider when planning the budget. For example, there will be a cost just to bring your yard back to its original condition. Will shrubs be removed? Will trucks tear up the lawn? Will trees need to be cut? In all cases, you'll have to spend money just to re-create what you already have.

If you want to sell your house immediately after finishing the addition, this may be an opportune time to create a better landscape for the entire home that will enhance its resale value. To do this, you should add ten or fifteen percent of the appraised value of the house to the construction-loan request to cover the costs of landscaping. If you have already put a good amount of work into your landscape over the past few years, you will need less than that amount. Also, if your landscape is already all that it should be and repair is all that interests you, then five, ten, even up to fifteen percent of the addition's cost could

be adequate. This, of course, largely depends on the extent of the damage done in the process of building the addition.

Adding On for Resale in Five to Ten Years

You can expect to invest about the same amount of money for re-landscaping for this situation as you would for adding on for immediate resale. When you're putting an addition on a building that you are planning on selling within five to ten years, it is likely that the construction is the result of a pressing need. You may

If you are not planning to immediately resell your home, it is more economical to install small plantings (A) with the goal of having them reach maturity (B) before you are ready to sell.

be adding a bedroom because of a new child, or a relative might be coming to live with you. If you are not ready simply to sell the house and buy a bigger one to accommodate your new extra space requirements, this strategy makes perfect sense.

As previously mentioned, construction damage to the existing landscape needs to be considered before you begin work. Established plants that can be saved should be set aside for reuse after construction. Mature trees need to be protected from damage and hardscape features in the immediate area, such as stone walls, wooden fencing, walkways, bluestone patios, or sculptures, need to be removed and replaced after all construction has taken place. In some circumstances, you may want to set aside any good-quality existing loam.

After the addition has been built, you can either replace the landscaping that had been there or you can make improvements that can add to the total value. An advantage in waiting for five to ten years before reselling the house is that you can use smaller plants, which cost less than larger ones. You do not need an immediate visual impact since you are not selling the house immediately. The lower cost of plantings will have a big impact on the return you get on money invested in plantings. A strategically placed tree that is only two inches in caliper may only cost a couple hundred dollars if planted professionally. A six-inch-caliper tree, however, will cost several times that. Eventually the two-inch tree will become the six-inch tree and your investment is far less because of the tree's growth and your patience.

For guidelines on adding on for resale in ten to thirty years or adding on to a permanent residence (retirement or dream house), see the corresponding sections under "Building a New House" on pages 37–40. The guidelines are much the same.

Renovating an Existing House

When we think of renovation, we often associate it with older homes in need of a face-lift. Perhaps you're considering the purchase of an older home, or maybe you just bought one. In some cases you may want to upgrade the existing landscape. Regardless of your situation or motivation, you must acquire appropriate financing before you begin this process.

If you're considering purchasing an older home that needs fixing up, it's important to be aware of all the costs before shopping for a mortgage.

Renovating for Immediate Resale

In this scenario there are three predominant possibilities. First, you're considering an older house and want to upgrade the landscape along with the renovation. Second, you want to upgrade the landscape in your present older home. Third, you wish to renovate your home and landscape at the same time for greater resale value. In all three cases, an appraisal of the house would make excellent fiscal sense. These scenarios all use a formula of five to fifteen percent of the value of the house to optimize your return on your investment in the landscaping. The reason for the broad range of the suggested investment in the landscape is the fact that an older home may already have established landscape features that have already added value. In a new home most of these same features will likely need to be added. This alone is a good reason for saving existing mature trees during the construction process.

We suggest that in landscaping a property for quick sale you use the bulk of your budget on mature trees, hardscape features, and plantings of shrubs and flowers that will make an immediate visual impact. Mature trees offer a sense of stability that can give prospective home buyers a sense of security. Hardscape features like walks and patios will add to the usability of the home and the land surrounding it. They also help buyers visualize how they will use the landscape. Shrubs and other plants such as perennial and annual flowers can add both color and fragrance — like a Realtor's technique of having the home seller bake an apple pie and leave it out to cool. Olfactory and visual stimuli are subtle but powerful.

When you're renovating a landscape, be sure to select plants and features that are appropriate to the style of your house. Foundation-style plantings do not complement a Victorial-style house.

Another consideration in the renovation of a home and its property is the historical context of the garden and the architecture. For example, if you are living in a Victorian home that has an overgrown or inappropriate foundation planting design, you may choose to replace it with one that is appropriate to the Victorian era. This may add even more value to the residence. Always be sure to consult a landscape design professional before embarking on this type of renovation — it requires special design skills and knowledge.

For guidelines on renovating for resale in five to ten years, see the corresponding section under "Adding On to an Existing House" on pages 40–41.

Renovating for Resale in Ten to Thirty Years

If your goal is resale farther down the road, then your landscape renovation can take place over several years. Most of the considerations for planting over an extended time have been covered previously. There are certain horticultural practices, however, that need to be considered if you are going to achieve your goal of having a balanced and consistent appearance at the time of sale. Specifically, when mixing mature plants with smaller nursery plants you need to consider the different rates of growth. Smaller plants of the same type that are being saved need to be encouraged in their growth, and there needs to be an established maintenance schedule to keep the growth of the larger existing plants in check. This provides a balanced, uniform landscape at the time that you are ready to sell.

For guidelines on renovating a permanent residence (retirement or dream house), see the corresponding section under "Building a New House" on page 39.

How to Finance Landscape Design and Construction

Here are some of the more common sources for financing landscaping services. These ideas may lead you to other ideas of how to be creative with your financing. Remember to take full advantage of what you have and to use lenders' money wisely! (We call our set of financing tips "green financial guidelines" to remind you that sometimes money *does* grow on trees.)

Green Financial Guideline (GFG) #1: *If you have the money, use it*

Any bank loan will cost you more interest than you can earn in an interest-bearing savings account. However, if you have money invested in stocks or mutual funds, you may wish to use this money as collateral for a loan. This will help avoid any capital gains that could result from a sale of these assets. Some exceptions to the above GFG are:

- If you have money invested in a tax-free municipal bond
- If you qualify for a low-interest government or utility company loan
- If you have to hold money in reserve for an anticipated need

GFG #2: *If you decide you need a loan, be sure to shop around*

Sources to explore include:

- HUD (Housing and Urban Development)
- FHA (Farmer's Home Administration)
- Home equity loan (line of credit)
- Credit union
- Whole life insurance policy
- Negotiate a lower interest rate on a loan with the bank that holds your assets
- Refinance an existing mortgage
- Take out a second mortgage
- Construction loan

GFG #3: *If you decide against a standard loan and you do not have enough money available, you may wish consider other sources of capital*

These sources include:

- Private loans
- Friends
- Relatives
- Institutional investors
- Sale of personal property
- Credit cards

6

Designing Your Landscape for Maximum Value

~

Have you ever walked out into your yard, looked around, and said to yourself, "I wish I had a better-looking yard, but I don't know *how* to make it look better?" After saying this, you go on about your business and yet you still haven't done anything about your yard. Why? It is usually because you simply don't know where to begin.

The first step in the process of creating a more appealing yard or landscape is the design. The design is nothing more than a plan that acts as a road map to help you get to where you want to go. In order to make your "map" you must go through a design process. Creating your own landscape design is very difficult and time consuming, and requires extensive knowledge. Although it appears that it should be one of the simplest things you could ever do, that definitely is not the case.

Landscaping involves a great deal more than plunking some shrubs down in front of a building or putting up a fence and placing some bushes in front of it. Good landscape design is about creating and defining an emotionally appealing and functional space with a variety of objects that work in harmony with each other. This harmony is not only visual but also cultural, in that the physical needs of all of the plants are being met — water, light, and so forth. On top of all this, the designed space needs to be structurally sound and provide a safe environment for living.

Developing the Design Yourself

The best landscape designers are people who have a thorough understanding of a variety of professional disciplines: civil engineering (surveying), horticulture (plants), agronomy (study of soils), entomology (insects), pathology (diseases), ecology (environmental interrelationships), mechanical or structural engineering (construction), and aesthetics. Some designers may also specialize in a particular style or approach to landscaping. For instance, a designer may choose to focus on Japanese gardens. There are five separate styles of Japanese gardens that a designer needs to understand in order to be proficient at designing those types of spaces.

This is not to say that you can't do an excellent job at designing your home landscape. But you need to be aware of what you are getting yourself into. Some of the most talented professional landscape designers gained their first experience designing their own properties. If you choose to design the landscape yourself, this chapter will help you chart that course. You will also want to refer to other publications and periodicals that elaborate on different approaches to the design process (see "For Further Reading" on page 159).

This chapter focuses on aspects of design that will help to increase the value of the space surrounding your home. If you are planning on using a professional designer, this chapter will help him or her do a better job for you. It will help to organize your thinking as well as give some insights into your wants and needs.

Questions to Ask About How Your Landscape Is Used

One of the first things that you need to do is organize your thinking in terms of your personal wants and needs. The best approach is to begin with the basic questions that you are likely to ask yourself in the design process:

- What elements are essential to have in your new landscape?
- What elements would you wish for in the ideal landscape?

It is always difficult to distinguish between features that we want and ones that we truly need. One way of sorting this out is to compile a list of everything that you could possibly want or need in your yard and landscaping (see the sample list on page 46). Use this list to solicit the input of all the people who will be using your yard frequently, as well. A good way to do this is to make copies of your list and have all users mark their own preferences and priorities.

This process will help to eliminate some things and to prioritize others. You can't satisfy everyone's desires, but you will have a pretty clear idea of the direction to take to meet almost everyone's needs. If you plan on reselling the house in the near future (one to six years), you need to keep in mind how likely it is that prospective buyers will want the same features you are choosing. In the end, if you create a landscape that is perfectly suited only to yourself and others who share your exact tastes, you limit the market of potential buyers. Unusual design elements can actually become a deterrent to selling and decrease the property value. If, however, you are planning on staying in this location for the long term, then the value you add is measured only by your own personal tastes.

WHAT DO YOU WANT IN YOUR LANDSCAPE?

An Assessment Tool

The list at right will help you assess the landscaping needs and wants of the people using your property. Some of these options are more likely to be viewed as essential to others (potential future buyers of your home); we've added asterisks to these elements.

To use this list, direct participants to rate each landscaping element on a scale of 1 to 5, with 1 being *most desirable,* 3 being *neutral,* and 5 being *least desirable.* For example, a rating of 1 beside "Deck" means a deck is one of the things you must have in your yard, while a 4 beside "Bird feeder" means you're not very excited about having birds in your yard, and a 5 beside it may indicate you hate birds (and the mess they can make).

To tally the results, make a separate list of all the elements that received a rating of 1 or 2 and note the ones that are asterisked (most appealing to a great number of people). This is your "shopping list" of priorities and individual items that you need as well as items that you want for your landscape.

Rate each landscape element on a scale of 1–5
(1 = most desirable, 5 = least desirable)

Annual flowers*	____	Outside shower/	
Apiary/beekeeping	____	changing area	____
Arbor/pergola*	____	Parking*	____
Barbecue	____	Patio*	____
Basketball court/hoop	____	Perennial flowers	____
Bird sanctuary	____	Picnic tables	____
Birdhouse/bird feeder*	____	Playhouse	____
Cold frames	____	Pond	____
Compost bin	____	Porch*	____
Cut-flower garden	____	Preserve existing	
Deck*	____	features	____
Doghouse/run/		Putting green	____
invisible fence	____	Raised garden	____
Drainage (drip edge,		Resale value*	____
wet areas, etc.)*	____	Rock garden	____
Dust reduction*	____	Rose garden	____
Fall color*	____	Sandbox	____
Fences*	____	Sculpture	____
Foundation plantings*	____	Shade trees*	____
Fountains	____	Small fruits (e.g., grapes,	
Fragrance*	____	blueberries, kiwis)	____
Garage*	____	Spring-flowering bulbs*	____
Garden bench*	____	Stone walls*	____
Gazebo/cupola	____	Storage shed*	____
Good view from house*	____	Summer-flowering bulbs	____
Good view of house		Swimming pool*	____
from street (important		Swing set	____
for resale value)*	____	Timber walls	____
Grassy sports area	____	Treehouse	____
Greenhouse	____	Vegetable garden	____
Ground cover		Vistas (mountain, river,	
(alternative to lawn)*	____	lake, ocean, etc.)*	____
Hammock/lounge chairs	____	Visual barrier (from	
Handicap accessible	____	traffic, street, or	
Hedges	____	neighbors)	____
Herb garden	____	Wading pool	____
Horseshoes field	____	Walkways*	____
Hot tub/Jacuzzi*	____	Water gardens	____
Lawn*	____	Well	____
Lighting*	____	Wildflower meadow	____
Low-maintenance garden*	____	Wildlife sanctuary	____
Multilevel decking*	____	Windbreaks*	____
Noise reduction	____	Winterscape	____
Orchard	____	Other: _____	____

Dividing Outdoor Space into "Rooms"

Another question you need to ask yourself is how you want to define the space. One of the best ways to do this is to think of the space in terms you can relate to, such as rooms of a house. This metaphor can help you understand where you can apply the items you have chosen to become part of your landscape. Therefore, ask this question: **What sort of "rooms" do you want to create?**

To understand the space outside your home, it's sometimes a good idea to think of it as the space you have inside your home — that is, of course, rooms, and how they are defined by the ways you use them. The rooms in our homes fall into three major categories:

- Private areas (den, bedroom, library)
- Public areas (living room, dining room)
- Service or utility areas (laundry room, kitchen)

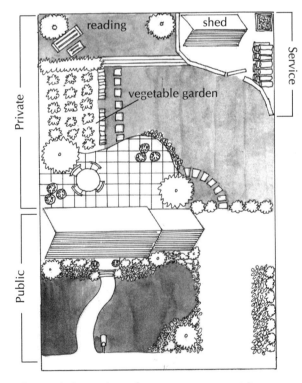

In determining what elements you want in your landscape, it's helpful to distinguish among its public, private, and service areas.

By more clearly defining the spaces that we have in our landscape, we can more clearly focus on how those spaces will be used.

Camouflage Areas

As part of your landscape planning, you also want to consider the things that you don't want to see there. Therefore, ask yourself: **Where are the "ugly" areas that you want to hide?**

In all landscapes, there are areas that will be unsightly because of their use. This could include areas where neighbors are visible, service areas, or a feature that distracts you from a beautiful view. By camouflaging these areas, you can enhance the beauty of your landscape. You can screen them in a variety of ways — with lattices, vines, fences, walls, hedges, trees, or water.

A bulky air-conditioning unit can distract from an otherwise attractive landscape. Camouflaging the unit with plantings prevents this effect.

WHAT AREAS DO YOU WANT TO SCREEN OR CAMOUFLAGE IN YOUR LANDSCAPE?

A CHECKLIST

If you have been living in one place for a while, you may not be aware of all of the unsightly views because you have become used to them. The following list will help you identify some of those distracting features. Check off the features that you need to hide.

Boat	_____	Neighbors/buildings	_____
Bulkheads	_____	Parked cars	_____
Clothesline	_____	Radio towers	_____
Commercial developments	_____	School yard/playing children	_____
Compost bin	_____	Septic tank/leach fields	_____
Dogs/animals	_____	Streetlight	_____
Electric meter	_____	Telephone poles and guy wires	_____
Electrical tranformers	_____	Traffic noise	_____
Garbage bins	_____	Traffic/road	_____
Gas or oil tanks	_____	TV satellite dish	_____
Industrial noise	_____	Well	_____
Landfill/gravel pit	_____	Woodpiles	_____

Choosing Types of Gardens

To continue to define the space that is called your landscape, you should also ask yourself: **Are there certain types of gardens that you would like to have?**

Consider the vast array of styles or types of gardens you can use in your yard. One thing you do need to consider in this regard, however, is the context of that garden in relation to the architecture of the building as well as to the neighborhood. If it doesn't "fit in with the theme," so to speak, the garden may not be appropriate to use — for example, foundation plants around a Japanese-style home or, conversely, a Japanese garden around a New England saltbox. You do not have to exclude their use, but remember that this may lower the perceived value of the property for a potential future buyer of your property.

Gardens are usually categorized into two major types: aesthetic and functional. *Aesthetic gardens* may be visually pleasing, aromatic, and/or theme oriented. *Functional gardens* are more practical in nature and are usually produce oriented, such as a vegetable garden. The following list provides some ideas for you to consider when making your choice.

WHAT KIND OF GARDENS DO YOU WANT?

A CHECKLIST

Following is a list of a wide variety of garden possibilities for your home landscape. Check off all those that you would like to have.

Productive Gardens

Basket Weaver's
    Garden   ____
Christmas Trees   ____
Cutting Garden   ____
Dye Garden   ____
Hayfield   ____
Herb Garden   ____
Low-Maintenance
    Vegetable Garden   ____
Medicinal Garden   ____
Orchard   ____
Perennial Vegetable
    Garden (asparagus,
    rhubarb, etc.)   ____
Permaculture   ____
Small Fruit Garden   ____
Vegetable Garden   ____
Weaver's Garden   ____
Woodlot   ____

Aesthetic Gardens

Alpine Garden   ____
Annual Flower Garden   ____
Bird Sanctuary   ____
Bog Garden   ____
Bulb Garden   ____
Cactus Garden   ____
Chinese Garden   ____
Colonial Garden   ____
Dried Flower Garden   ____
Dwarf Conifer Garden   ____
English Cottage Garden   ____
Fall Color Garden   ____
Fern Garden   ____
Fragrance Garden   ____
French Parterre   ____
"G" Scale Railroad
    Garden   ____
Hanging Garden   ____
Hidden Garden   ____

Hosta Garden   ____
Italian Garden   ____
Japanese Garden   ____
Lily Garden   ____
Maze   ____
Meditation Garden   ____
Moon Garden   ____
Particular Color Garden   ____
Perennial Flower Garden   ____
Oriental Garden   ____
Rock Garden   ____
Rose Garden   ____
Shade Garden   ____
Shrubbery Garden   ____
Silver Garden   ____
Victorian Garden   ____
Water Garden   ____
Wildflower Garden   ____
Winter Garden   ____
Woodland Garden   ____

Planning for the Future

You also need to consider what you anticipate happening to your home and landscape in the future. A couple of good questions to ask yourself: **How long do you plan on living in your home before you sell? Do you plan any additions to your home soon?**

When you consider planning your landscape, you must also think about how your family's needs may change. For example, you could want a swimming pool in a few years when the children are older. In this case, you wouldn't want to put a patio where the pool is likely to go. Nor would you plant a tree that eventually will grow over the area, casting shade and dropping leaves into the water.

WHAT DO YOU ANTICIPATE AS YOUR FUTURE LANDSCAPING NEEDS?

A CHECKLIST

Here is a list of a number of possible changes that you might make on your property in the future. To help you anticipate future landscaping needs, check off those that apply.

Additions to the house   ____
Children   ____
Children coming to live at home   ____
Elderly parents   ____
Expanded family   ____
Garage   ____
Housing developments   ____
New pets   ____
Rights-of-way:
   Electric   ____
   Gas   ____
   Water   ____
   Access (property or shoreline)   ____
Road expansion   ____
Swimming pool   ____
Other: _____

WHAT HARDSCAPING ELEMENTS DO YOU WANT IN YOUR LANDSCAPE?

AN ASSESSMENT TOOL

Use a rating system of 1 to 5 to assess how important each of the following hardscaping elements is to you, with 1 being "must have," 2 being "would like to have," and 5 being "prefer not to have." After you've done this, find the elements you've rated 1 or 2 and note which ones have letters in parentheses. These indicate what materials those features could be built from (see "Materials Key" below). Circle the letter or letters that indicate the material(s) you prefer. For example, if you need a retaining wall made of fieldstone, the rating would be 1 FdSt; if you'd like to have two freestanding walls (one made of brick and the other made of quarry stone), the rating would be 2 ClBr, QSt.

MATERIALS KEY

Bmb:	**Bamboo**	Grv:	**Gravel**
BkMl:	**Bark Mulch**	LdsTmb:	**Landscape**
Blst:	**Bluestone**		**Timbers**
CmBl:	**Cement Block**	Mtl:	**Metal**
CmBr:	**Cement Brick/**	MtlP:	**Metal Pipe**
	Paver	PFr:	**Palm Fronds**
ClBr:	**Clay Brick**	PtoCn:	**Patio Concrete**
Cn:	**Concrete**	PSt:	**Pea Stone**
CrSt:	**Crushed Stone**	Pl:	**Plastic**
FdSt:	**Fieldstone**	QSt:	**Quarry Stone**
Flst:	**Flagstone**	RJ:	**River Jack**
FlFdst:	**Flat Fieldstone**	TC:	**Terra-cotta**
Gl:	**Glass**	Wd:	**Wood**
Grn:	**Granite**	Wlr:	**Wrought Iron**

Hardscaping Element	Desirability Rating (1–5)	Preferred Material (circle one)
Arbor/pergola	_____	Wd/FdSt/QSt/ClBr/Bmb/Pl/CmBl/MtlP
Awning	_____	Wd/Bmb/Pl/PFr
Cold frame	_____	Wd/Pl/Gl
Decks:		
Single level	_____	Wd
Dual level	_____	
Multilevel	_____	
Drip edges/roof drainage	_____	Wd/ClBr/BlSt/Grn/Tc/CrSt/PSt/Grv/RJ
Drainage	_____	Pl/MtlP/CrSt/Grv
Fences	_____	Wd/ClBr/Bmb/Cn/Wlr/Mtl
Screening:		
Accent	_____	Wd/FdSt/QSt/ClBr/LdsTmb/Bmb/CmBl/MtlP/Gl
Sleeve	_____	
Perimeter	_____	
Gazebo/cupola	_____	Wd/Pl/Gl
Greenhouse	_____	Pl/MtlP
Irrigation	_____	Wd/FdSt/QSt/ClBr/Grn/Bmb/TC/Pl/MtlP/Gl/Cn
Lighting	_____	Wd/QSt/ClBr/CmBr/Flst/BlSt/FlFdSt/PtoCn/Grn/CrSt/PSt/Grv/Cn
Patio	_____	Wd/LdsTmb/Grn/Pl/MtlP/Cn
Poles/posts:		
Flag	_____	Wd/FdSt/QSt/ClBr/BlSt/PtoCn/LdsTmb/Grn/TC/Pl/CmBl/Gl/Cn
Hitching	_____	
Mailbox	_____	
Other	_____	
Pots/containers	_____	Wd/FdSt/QS/ClBr/CmBr/LdsTmb/Grn/CmBr/Cn
Raised beds	_____	Wd/FdSt/QSt/ClBr/Grn/Bmb/PFr/CmBl/MtlP/Cn
Ramada/shade house	_____	Wd/FdSt/QSt/ClBr/BlSt/Grn/Bmb/Cn
Seating	_____	Wd/FdSt/QSt/ClBr/Grn/Bmb/TC/Gl/Cn
Statues	_____	Wd
Structures:		
Birdhouse	_____	Wd/QSt/ClBr/CmBr/FlSt/BlSt/FlFdSt/PtoCn/Grn/CrSt/PSt/Grv/
Playhouse	_____	BkMl/Cn
Treehouse	_____	
Storage shed	_____	
Woodshed	_____	
Outhouse	_____	
Pool house	_____	
Other	_____	
Walks:		
Formal	_____	FdSt/Qst/ClBr/CmBr/LdsTmb/Grn/CmBl/Cn
Informal	_____	
Walls:		
Freestanding	_____	FdSt/QSt/ClBr/Grn/Pl/CmBl/Cn
Retaining	_____	
Water garden	_____	
Swimming pool	_____	

Creating Halls, Walls, and Walks to Connect Your Outdoor "Rooms"

Now that you've identified the particular rooms and areas you would like included in your landscape, think about how they will be defined in relation to each other. Just as the rooms in your house need to be separate yet connected, the rooms in your yard need similar definition. This can be done through the use of stone walls, fences, and brick paths, to name a few elements of "hardscaping," the nonliving component of the landscape. The hardscaping assessment tool on the previous pages gives some of the different types of partitions and walks you can use for your outdoor rooms. In addition to this list of hardscape items, there is a supplemental list of possible materials that can be used for building many of these elements.

Selecting Colors for Your Landscape

The colors you choose for your landscape can be influential in creating balance and continuity. Colors can be used to establish a theme or a common thread that unifies the garden as well. Remember, though, when choosing colors, to consider the present color of your home, and any plans you have to change that color in the future; coordinate the plantings accordingly. For example, if you have a white home, you wouldn't want to use white flowering shrubs, because they would not create enough contrast.

DETERMINING COLOR PREFERENCES

AN ASSESSMENT TOOL

Rate your preferences for using each of the following colors in your landscape using a scale of 1 to 5 (1 being the most desired and 5 the least).

Blue	_____	Red	_____
Bright colors	_____	Rose	_____
Brown	_____	Silver	_____
Orange	_____	Yellow	_____
Pastel colors	_____	White	_____
Pink	_____	Other colors	_____
Purple	_____		

Hardscaping includes the nonliving components of your landscaping, such as pathways, benches, planters, decks, and fences, to name just a few.

A possible exception might be a broad-leaved evergreen with white blooms. If the bloom period is relatively short, the effect of the dark evergreen against the white home is dramatic.

Drawing a Plot Plan

To begin the process of actually putting your landscape plan down on paper, you will need a plot plan of the property. Such a plan may already exist, especially if it's a new home. Find out before starting. It may save a lot of time and money.

This plan helps you to map out where everything is located. This is important, because in order to place new features, you need to know where the existing features are.

If you are unable to locate an existing plan, here are the steps to follow to draft your own plot plan.

1. Establish a scale. This will enable you to draw all the features on the plan in the same relationship as they exist in your yard. A convenient scale is one inch equals eight feet (1:8 scale). This means that one inch on your plan will equal eight feet in your yard. If one page is not large enough, break your yard down into sections such as front yard, backyard, side yard, pool area, etc.

2. Locate existing features. These features include the exterior walls of your home, with windows, doorways, and vents clearly marked. Walkways, drives, parking, and service entries should also be included on this plan. If you have trees, shrubs, or other landscape

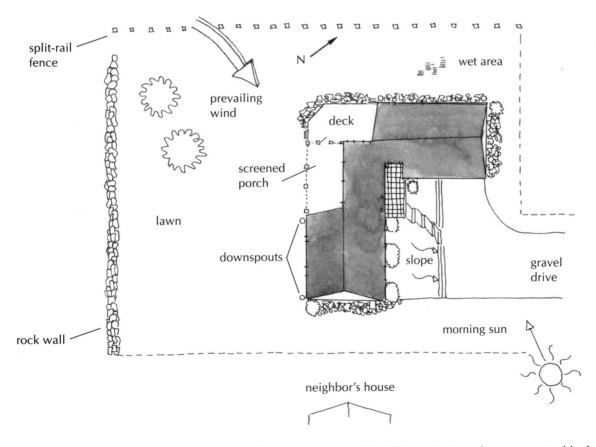

You will need a plot plan of your property (drawn to scale) with all the existing elements noted before you can begin mapping out new features you want to add.

features that will be staying in their present locations, you should indicate them as well. Don't forget areas such as rocky outcrops, slopes, and wet spots; they should be mapped as well (see the section below on "Lay of the Land").

Locate Lay-of-the-Land Features

The lay of the land of your property has a major impact on your final design. It determines what individual features will be used, and where they will be located in your landscape. For example, it would be a mistake to put a swimming pool on a rocky outcrop or under a large tree. There are many features that should be considered as you look at the existing terrain. On your plan, try to mark areas that are rocky, low-lying, wet, windy, or shady, and be sure to display other distinct features that need to be taken into account as you plan your landscaping.

The physical properties of the site can also affect the growing conditions for your plants. If you locate a tree on the shady side of the house, the chances are that it will bloom later, and its growth cycle will be slower than that of a tree planted in a sunny location. Another example of a site condition affecting the growth of plants is the proximity of a large body of water. This will generally have a warming influence on the air, because the water acts as a solar mass. This will allow you to grow plants that might otherwise be considered only marginally hardy to the area in which you live.

The weather can also influence your plan. Knowing the amount and frequency of rainfall, the number of frost-free days, and the "hardiness zone" of your home will help to determine what kinds of plants you'll be able to include in your plan. A USDA Hardiness Zone Map is in Appendix 2. Use this map to help you determine the zone you live in. Your local nursery/

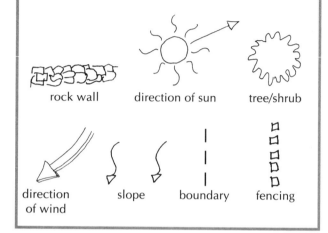

LANDSCAPE SYMBOLS

It's important that you adopt a consistent set of landscape symbols to make items easier to recognize on your plan. Here are some typical symbols used on landscape plans.

rock wall   direction of sun   tree/shrub

direction of wind   slope   boundary   fencing

LAY-OF-THE-LAND FEATURES TO CONSIDER IN DESIGNING YOUR LANDSCAPE

Bodies of water
Boulders
Dappled shade
Deep shade
Drainage problems
Erosion
Existing drainage pipes
Existing paths
Flat terrain
Full sun
Grove of willow trees
Large trees
Ledge
Low-lying areas
Physical structures
Poor air circulation
Poor grass growth
Rocky outcrops
Septic tank/leach field location
Slopes
Wet areas
Windy areas

garden center will be a valuable resource to help you select plants for your yard that will grow in your hardiness zone. The two weather indicators that we recommend putting on your plot plan are the direction of the prevailing winds and an arrow indicating north or south.

Understanding Basic Aesthetic Principles of Design

The way that all your landscaping elements fit together can be beautiful, mediocre, ugly, or even a combination. The overall perception of your landscape is not determined so much by what individual elements you have put into place as it is by how well everything is placed in the space. If you don't have a good sense of the dynamics of the space and how the objects interact, it is unlikely that your final landscape will be very attractive.

There are a variety of ways of looking at space. In Asia, designers tend to see the space as being defined by the objects within the space. In general, Europeans (and Americans) tend to view space in terms of the objects individually, rarely considering the dynamic relationships between objects.

By developing an understanding and appreciation of how objects interact in space, you will greatly improve your ability to decide what shapes and sizes of objects should be placed where in the landscape. We hope that this basic overview of generally accepted principles of good aesthetics will give you a useful foundation for looking at and planning your landscape design.

Create Balance

There are essentially two types of balance: formal and informal. Traditional landscapes in our part of the world primarily use formal balance, which is characterized by two sides that reflect each other exactly. That is, if you drew a line through the center of the composition, the two sides would be mirror reflections of each other. Good examples of classic formally balanced landscapes are a French parterre and the allée of trees lining the road approaching a mansion in the Old South style. Most formally balanced landscapes use a square or rectangle as a basis for establishing the desired balance.

Informal balance is the tradition for Asian gardens and landscapes, and is based on designs found in nature. Japanese and Chinese landscapes are good examples of this approach. Most informally balanced landscapes

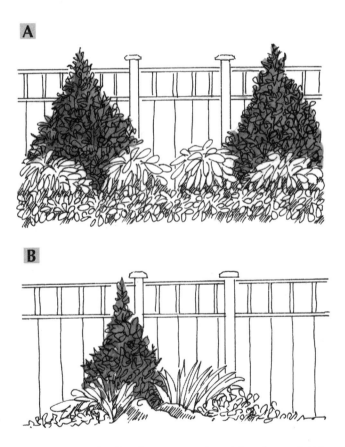

Balance in the landscape can be either formal (A), with the two sides that are exact reflections of each other, or informal (B), which is based on a more natural-looking design.

use a triangle as a basis for establishing the desired balance.

A balanced landscape feels more comfortable to look at because it is "secure" and doesn't feel disjointed. It also imparts a feeling of being finished and established. A balanced landscape is usually an indication that some forethought has gone into the design of a space.

The Impact of Framing

If you have ever had a photograph or painting professionally matted and framed, you are aware of the powerful impact that good framing can have on a viewed scene. Professional photographers use natural framing as a way of capturing images to give them a greater sense of depth. If you look at a photo of a barn sitting in a field, it feels as though it is floating there in space with nothing more to anchor it to earth than the field itself. What if the photo were taken from a perspective that included the trunk

Trees and other vertical elements in the landscape should be used to "frame" the view from your yard. This increases both the impact and the intimacy of the view.

of a tree on the left, a branch cutting across the sky above the barn scene, a grove of trees on the right, and a road in the foreground? In this way, the scene has been framed.

There are numerous opportunities to frame important aspects of your yard or property. The first priority is usually the view of the house or other building from the street. You have to consider how people are likely to look at the scene and from what angle. Try to remember that a frame is made up of four sides. Strong vertical elements such as trees or erect shrubs can be used for the left and right sides. Shrubs can be used for the bottom portion of the frame. The crowns of trees behind the house could serve as the top line of the frame.

A second area that can be captured by framing is the "vista" or viewed scenery. This is usually viewed from a deck or window or door. One of the biggest mistakes in creating a vista is to show the whole thing. By breaking it up with vertical lines you can create a series of pictures. One of our clients had a property with a magnificent view of Sebago Lake. We told her that the first thing that needed to be done was to plant some birch trees in front of it. She was in shock. Then we explained our objective and promised her that if she wasn't satisfied, we would take the trees away and put in a new lawn. When the work was finished, she understood what was happening and relished the series of views seen from many different viewpoints.

Informally balanced landscapes can be a lot trickier to frame. In order to understand how it is done best, you need to consider design techniques developed by the Japanese. The basic approach is called "capturing alive that which is beyond." One of the most intriguing approaches is to combine context and scale. By placing two duplicate or similar objects in two separate environments you are given a sense of continuity of design. For example, if there is a certain type of tree on a neighbor's property, put one of the same type of tree on your own property. If there is water in the distance, make it part of the foreground or midground by adding a water feature.

The Importance of Contrast

Contrast in a landscape is created where objects, shapes, or lines are differentiated from each other and there is an overall better visual understanding of those aspects. If used properly, it can really make a landscape come alive. Contrast can be achieved through lines, forms, colors, textures, and objects. For example, a landscape with a single consistent hue of one color of green would lack contrast and appear to be flat. By introducing different hues of green, you have maintained context while still using contrast. A landscape made up entirely of horizontal lines would be monotonous. By imposing strong vertical lines at a variety of distances, you would create a dynamic landscape with great depth.

Contrast can be taken to extremes and create a sense of disharmony, so a word of caution is in order. If you have a bed of flowers of warm orange hues and you place a purple flower in their midst, it could be terribly disconcerting to the eye. Unless your objective is disharmony, avoid the use of contrast simply for contrast's sake. There should be an element of harmony associated with contrasting elements.

You can add interest and contrast to your landscape by introducing hardscaping elements (such as the fence) and plantings of varying heights, colors, leaf forms, and textures.

Create Context

Context in landscape design can be defined as having a clearly established relationship among outward appearances. If your house had Victorian-style architecture with a Chinese-style garden, the garden would be said to be "out of context" with the architecture. You can also have an object within the garden that is out of context with the rest of the plantings. If you have a theme garden that is based on native plants and you feature a non-native plant, that plant is out of context. It can also apply on a larger scale.

This desert-style landscape is out of context with the clapboard house, and with the other yards in the suburban neighborhood where it stands.

If you live in a neighborhood that has a consistent style and approach to landscape design and you do something entirely different, your landscape is out of context with the neighborhood.

Appropriate use of context shows forethought in the execution of the design and provides a consistency that can create a peaceful feeling.

Use a Sense of Depth

Depth is relatively easy to impart to a landscape design. Depth in the garden is achieved by understanding and creating foreground, midground, and background. A background can act as a stage upon which the structures and the plantings are set. The foreground is a defining element that helps to set the limits of the space. The scale and placement of the midground objects or elements help to indicate the amount of depth. A sense of depth can be achieved in a relatively narrow plane through "cascading" the objects. Think

of an eight-foot solid fence with plantings placed in front of it that are massed together and stand three feet tall. Directly in front of these plantings is another fence that has an open picket style and is two feet in height. Directly in front of this fence is a mass of perennials eight inches in height. Adjacent to the perennials is a line of stones or bricks that are three inches tall. In front of the stones or bricks you find a pathway. The distance between the walk and the fence is no more than three feet, yet you have created a considerable sense of depth. The foreground is the walk and the background is the solid fence. The midground is defined by the cascading elements that are between the two.

Create Visual Flow

Visual flow is the way that the eye will move when it is viewing a scene or an object. The eye should be led through the landscape in a natural and easy sequence. If you find the landscape difficult to look at, it is usually because visual

In a relatively narrow landscape, you can create a sense of depth by layering elements in a cascading arrangement (A). In a larger landscape, use the full range of area (foreground, midground, and background) to project an inviting entranceway (B).

flow was not a consideration in the design. Another problem can occur when important aspects of the scene are not viewed — if the entry, exit, path, or destinations are not considered, the scene may not flow. If you think of the placement of objects as being steps and their relative placement and height in relation to each other as a staircase, you are more likely to grasp the

A

B

A landscape entryway that leads people naturally through it has good visual flow (A), while overgrown or poorly designed entryways are confusing and discourage people from entering (B).

application of visual flow as a natural progression for the eye. This in turn is related to physical flow, indicating where you want the person to actually move in the landscape.

Putting It All Together

By now you should have the following things accomplished:

1. Plot plan drawn to scale showing the existing features in your landscape.
2. Lists filled out and prioritized:
   - Wants and Needs
   - Rooms
   - Screening/camouflage
   - Garden use
   - Hardscape: walls, fences, walks, and their materials
   - Future changes
3. A basic understanding of the principles of aesthetics.

Review these lists and highlight with one color each of the items you've rated important — 1 or 2. Then highlight with a different color the items that you've ranked as a 3 priority, so it's easy to find your highest priorities.

You may find it beneficial at this time to make photocopies of your plot plan for making rough sketches. The alternative is to use tracing paper and make a series of overlays. Either way, you can experiment with different approaches to some of your high-priority items.

The Designing Process

Although there are as many different design processes as there are designers, the following procedure is one that can help to lead you through the entire design of the landscape logically. Using the assessment tools and checklist on pages 46–52:

1. Divide the property into rooms: service, public, and private. Once you're finished, you can start sketching out the rooms that will fit into those areas.

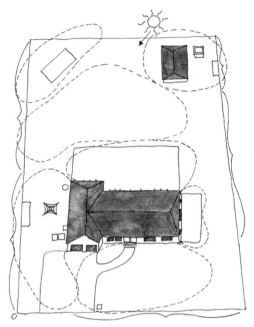

2. Determine screening/camouflage areas. Think about where your views will be and decide which areas you'll need to camouflage, or hide.

3. Decide what hardscaping elements you're going to need. Sketch in walls, halls, and walkways, using notes to yourself on what materials you intend to use.

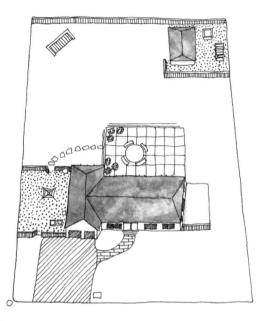

4. Anticipate future changes. Stop and consult your Future Changes list and see if there are any serious conflicts with your space allocations at this point, based on changes you anticipate for the future. If there are, redo your design to accommodate them. If not, then move on to the next step.

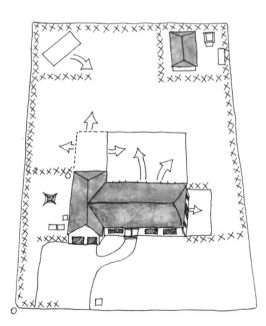

5. Consult your Wants and Needs list. Check to see if you've included all of your high-priority items in your design. If not, which of the rooms, halls, walls, or walkways are going to be best suited for them? Remember, at this point you're not overly concerned about exact measurements. Just try to fit all of your high-priority wants and needs comfortably into the spaces you've designed.

6. Add gardens. Once you're comfortable with the overall layout, take a look at the Gardens list. This is where you can set the tone, texture, or overall theme of the landscape. Some of the garden types fit comfortably into an individual room, whereas others may determine the style of architecture and ambience used for the outdoor areas. For instance, suppose you choose the following items as high priority: water, bridge, cupola/gazebo, stones. Then you look at the Gardens list and you decide upon a style of Chinese. This would influence the style of bridge, the cupola or gazebo, how you would use the water, and where to place the rocks. If you had chosen Japanese, the approach would be entirely different.

7. Apply the aesthetic principles. This may prove to be the most difficult aspect of the design, because it is subtle and relatively subjective. In order to create a landscape with longterm value to others, you need to avoid creating something only you would enjoy. Think of the various objects that you are using in terms of shapes and sizes. This will allow you to "sculpt" the space without being overly concerned about the particular objects.

8. Designate planting areas. Plants are used to fill out your outdoor rooms, provide focal points, framing, screening, and backdrops, and help lead the eye through the landscape. Place plants into your plan by designating them as plant types, such as trees, shrubs, perennials, annuals, bulbs, ground covers, and vines. Don't name the plants at this time; just label them according to their relative heights — very high, high, medium high, medium, medium low, low, and very low. Abbreviating these labels helps to save time and space. For instance, a medium-high shrub might be labeled "S,mh." Your final plant choices will be determined by a number of factors, including growth habit, color, texture, shade tolerance, degree of hardiness, soil type and moisture, relative maintenance, susceptibility to disease and insects, and availability.

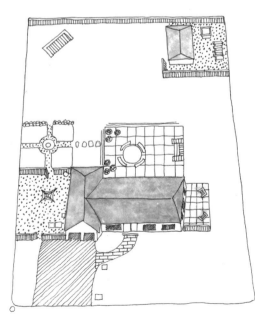

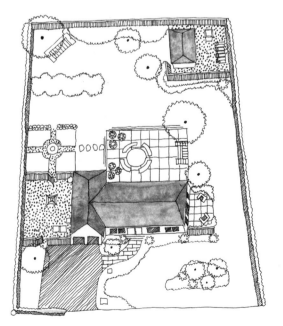

BASIC DESIGN TOOLS

- Three #2 pencils
- Compass for drawing circles
- ⅛-inch architect's scale (ruler)
- Five sheets of 8½ x 11⅛-inch ruled graph paper
- Landscape symbols template
- Eraser with brush
- Five sheets of tracing paper

Other helpful tools:
- Portable drafting board
- Measuring wheel
- 100-foot measuring tape
- 50-foot measuring tape
- Protractor
- Compass
- Pop level or string level
- French curve set (3 sizes)
- Koh-i-noor pen set
- Ames lettering guide
- Straightedge set (3 triangles of different shapes)
- Engineer's scale (6 scales) or architect's scale (6 scales)
- Gumby ruler (flexible edge)
- Template package (circles, squares, landscape, lines)
- Roll of tracing vellum, 24" x 30'
- Box of 24 color drawing pencils
- Spray fixative

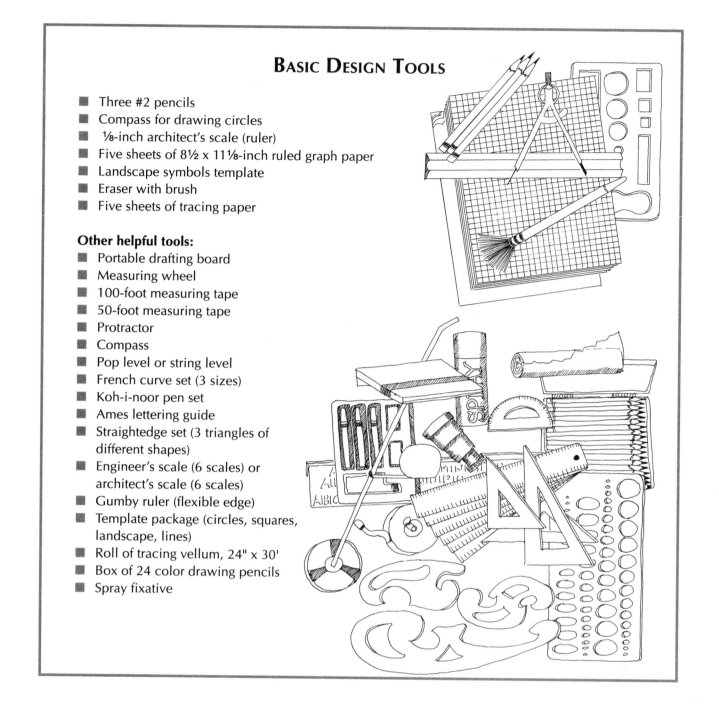

7

Investing in Hardscaping Elements

WHEN WE SPEAK OF HARDSCAPE, WE'RE talking about the part of your landscape that is not living. It's the part of the landscape we refer to as the "backbone" of your yard. Individual components might be stone or brick walls, fences, patios and walks, raised beds, arbors, and decks. Other elements seldom associated with hardscape but that do belong in this category are lighting, irrigation, statues, and pots. Also included are containers used for planters, cold frames for starting seedlings, and structures such as woodsheds, pool houses, and greenhouses. We consider plant-support materials like loam and mulch to be in this category.

Hardscape is a relatively new term describing basically everything in the landscape except for the plants. In this chapter, we'll discuss the elements of hardscape. By giving you details about each item, and suggestions about important construction details, you will learn what is a good job and what is not. Why do you need to have a batter on a stone retaining wall? What materials make for good walks? These are the types of questions you need to know the answers to if you want to get a quality job. The contractor you pick should know the answers — and a professional will! You will also learn what to look for during construction and what to expect from a finished product. For detailed and specific questions you should ask contractors, see chapter 12.

The value that hardscape adds can be significant. The difference between the value added by plants and the value added by hardscape is generally the effective return you can get on the dollar invested. With plants, you can work with small sizes that will grow and small quantities that you can divide and multiply. That means that your initial investment can be relatively little, and the worth at maturity can be substantially greater.

Hardscaping refers to elements such as walkways, arbors, patios, walls, and garden pools.

The hardscape acts like any property. It may depreciate in value immediately; therefore, it could be difficult to get an immediate positive monetary return. For instance, if you were to spend $3,000 on the installation of a walkway to your front door, it might not immediately add $3,000 in value to your home. Also, the quality of the construction can significantly affect the perceived value of any hardscape element. The quality will determine, in many cases, its longevity and therefore bring a better return, eventually, on money invested.

Types of Walls

There are two basic types of walls: freestanding and retaining. The reason for a freestanding wall (masons refer to them as "three-sided" walls) is usually to mark a boundary, or to add punctuation to a walk area or garden. In colonial times,

stone wall borders were a good way of making use of the rocks removed from fields. It's still a good way to use the stones today, when a patch of rocky ground needs to be cleared.

Here in Maine, we heard two farmers talking about this very subject. The first farmer commented, "There sure are a lot of stones in this field." The second farmer responded, "Ayuh." Curious, the first farmer asked, "Where'd they all come from?" Farmer Two said, "Glacier brought 'em." "Well, where'd the glacier go?" was the next question. "Back for more stones," was the response.

Retaining walls are referred to as "two-sided" walls (the top and facing sides). Unlike freestanding walls, these walls are often built on a slope to prevent erosion and provide a more solid foundation for an area of the landscape.

A retaining wall should always be built with its function in mind. For example, if a retaining wall is built to hold back earth for a terraced garden, it should be engineered to stay upright!

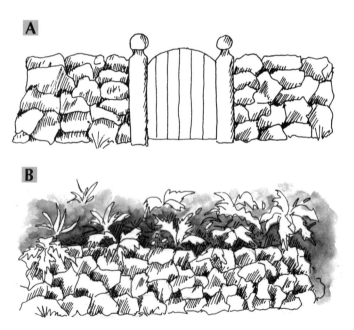

A freestanding wall (A) is most often used to mark a boundary or act as an entryway to a garden, while a retaining wall (B) is usually used to hold back earth and prevent erosion.

Too often we see poorly constructed retaining walls toppling over. This is usually because the proper engineering was never done and the dynamics of soil and water movement were not taken into consideration.

Another matter to consider is whether the wall is constructed using the dry-laid method or the wet (mortared) method. Ask your contractor if he or she has employees who can use the method that's right for your situation, and look at their work. And don't look at just pictures — go see the work in person. This could save you from picking an inexperienced mason. Many landscape contractors use an apprentice training program, and we recommend that you ask your prospective contractor about his or her training programs. (Good stonemasons are not born — they are trained by other good stonemasons.)

We believe that a dry-laid stone wall is superior to a mortared wall in many, if not most, situations. A dry-laid wall, when constructed correctly, can last for generations. The points of friction are very important for this method. Each stone placed in the wall should have enough other stones touching it to make both the weight and the friction points hold it together even when subjected to frost heaving year after year. Our mason describes this construction technique as allowing the wall to float and flex with the movement of the ground beneath. If you are not affected by frost, the decision is an aesthetic one. We still feel dry-laid walls may be your best value. Your local landscape or mason professional will have valuable experience and examples of walls of both constructions to show you. Another good reason for choosing a dry-laid wall is the relative ease of maintenance — repairs to a wet-laid wall are invariably more expensive and time consuming.

However, if you do choose a mortared or cemented wall, you should know about techniques

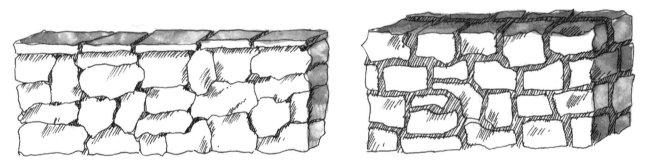

A dry-laid wall (left) is constructed with the stones touching each other, while a wet-laid wall (right) connects the stones together with mortar or cement.

Tips for Working with Stone

Buying Stone. Purchase your stone from a quarry; shop around for the best price. Check with your state or county government for lists of closed quarries. Their owners may be willing to let you pick your own stone.

Harvesting Stone. Find stone in the woods to use for walls and accents in gardens. When you harvest stone in the woods, be sure to have permission from the owner. It is illegal to pull stone walls down without written permission. If you are removing a boundary wall, you must get permission from both landowners.

that prevent or lessen water and frost damage, saving you maintenance problems and money. Generally, some kind of drainage footer or bed is needed, usually constructed with crushed stone, geotextile, and drainage pipe. It's not always necessary, but if you live in an area of frost or heavy soil, you need to allow water some type of exit, or your stone wall could fall over. In the case of wet-laid walls a technique using "weep holes" is essential — crushed stone wrapped in geotextile with small water-exit holes across the wall. The number of holes is determined by how much water accumulates at that spot.

The footing or base is also extremely important to the life of a wet-laid wall, whether it's constructed of stone, brick, or cement block. One method is to pour a base of concrete below the frost line. Expansion joints in the wall can also help. These joints allow parts of the wall to move independently of each other, so that the wall is not one large, brittle expanse but many smaller pieces of wall. The biggest drawback to this method is that after years of frost heaving, the sections may not settle back as originally constructed, giving the wall an uneven appearance. Another money-saving idea for a wet wall is to use cement block for the bulk of the wall, and then veneer stone to the wall's face. This method requires less stone, and if stone is scarce, it could ultimately save you money.

Walls: Value Added

Walls will add value to your property in two basic ways — aesthetics and function. A wall can add a feeling of balance, maturity, and permanence to a home. It evokes security and stability by making the viewer feel comfortable and safe. Regardless of the reason, though, it is essential that the basic character and design of the wall are consistent with the architectural style of the house.

There are some interesting ways you can make a wall unique. One way would be to build

When constructing a dry-laid retaining wall, you should use geotextile and crushed stone behind the wall to ensure good drainage without soil migration.

planter areas into it or give it plant pockets, so you can incorporate vines or perennials into the wall. Lichen on walls also appeals to many people. Manure tea, sour milk, or buttermilk painted on the stone will give the lichen a place to grow. Using large stones to create a vertical element in an otherwise horizontally built wall is also an interesting change of pace. Since each wall is its own work of art, each wall can have a character as individual as its owner's. Check with your builder for his or her ideas.

Options in Walkways, Paths, Terraces, and Patios

These four landscape components encompass a diverse group of materials. You may consider clay brick, bluestone, concrete paver, flat stone, or even cobblestone for the construction materials. You might think about walks as areas to the front and back door or you may want paving in different areas such as garden paths or arbor passages.

With any of these applications, you should consider frost and hydraulic damage when

Options for paving materials include (left to right): brick, concrete paver, bluestone, cobblestone, flat stone, and flagstone.

planning these walking or sitting areas. Your contractor should construct an adequate base to keep your paved areas from heaving, whether they are dry or wet laid. Keep in mind that unless you go below the frost line in your area, there will be some movement of the paving material, no matter what it is. The problem is that this could make it prohibitively expensive to install a flat surface outside.

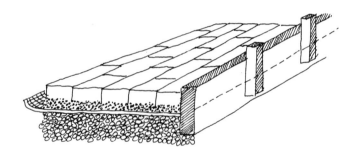

When constructing a walkway base, you should use geotextile, crushed stone, and stone dust to ensure adequate drainage and prevent heaving.

To minimize the heaving, your contractor can use several different methods. We recommend using crushed stone to give the water a place to go so it can then percolate down into the subsoils, and geotextile to keep the bed intact where the bricks or other stone will be set. Stone dust or concrete sand will compact for an excellent setting bed and correct compaction of all materials, so that the bricks and stones don't move around or shift when people are walking on them. The idea is to create a base that not only will repel large amounts of water but also will quickly move the inevitable moisture away from the bottom of your paved area. Some contractors use gravel in place of the crushed stone. This method has been employed for many years

with some success and is particularly good for driveways. Under walks and patios, we find the crushed stone to be superior, because it gives the frost a place to break up and the water an area to be collected. One note about this crushed stone — it must be sharp or have flat edges so it will compact. The same is true of the stone dust and sand. Imagine trying to compact ball bearings or marbles — the same concept applies to the stone or sand.

Your contractor should also understand about the use of edging, soldier rows, and sailor rows (see glossary for definitions). These features are used to keep your patios and walks from migrating or from separating. Plastic and aluminum edges are now used instead of soldier and sailor rows. These new edge inventions are very effective, but the purist will want to use the old-fashioned method.

Paved areas should also be relatively flat, with a pitch to allow positive drainage and a minimum of water pooling. This pitch can be so slight as to be indiscernible by eye (one percent or a ⅛-inch drop per foot is adequate).

In some cases it may be desirable to have your stone or bluestone material bound with plants such as creeping thyme or grass. This method is usually reserved for loose-laid, loam-based patios or walks in informal settings using larger individual paving units. The thyme actually has a preference for gravelly, well-drained soils beneath it. We don't recommend this method in heavy traffic areas, or areas likely to be shoveled in the winter. For these paved areas, it is not necessary to have an edge to prevent migration (paved-material movement). This would also be true if the area is mortared or wet laid.

When considering a wet-laid patio or walk, be aware of the potential for cracking from frost heaving. Make sure you have gone over the type of base with the contractor. You should also discuss its depth and the performance of other similarly constructed outside paved areas the contractor has done. No matter where you live, correctly installed drainage is an essential part

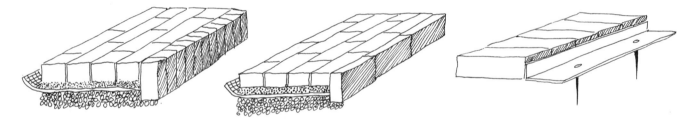

To keep patios and walkways from migrating or separating, be sure the edges are finished with one of these methods (left to right): soldier rows, sailor rows, or plastic or aluminum edging.

Tips for Working with Brick

Finding used brick. Look around for any demolition going on in your area or call a demolition company for information if you are interested in making a brick patio or walkway. It may have bricks to sell or may be willing to let you pick your own from a site. (A word of caution: Do not under any circumstances enter a demolition site without permission, a hard hat, and/or an escort.) Secondhand bricks will not last as long as new bricks, so consider this approach carefully. A good tip to delay the brick from shattering is to dip the entire brick in a good water sealant.

Use sealant. Sealing any brick or cement paver is a good idea. You can buy sealant from your local brick supplier or buy a nationally advertised brand. We always offer our customers the option of having their top surface sealed. Use a roller or spray the sealant for best results.

of this type of project. Dry or wet laid, north or south — without it, your paved area will shift, crack, and become a liability rather than the asset it should be.

Paths and Patios: Value Added

The value provided by these hardscape elements is, as with the walls, both functional and aesthetic. Functionally, paths and patios facilitate flow and physical movement through the landscape. These elements are practical and durable, providing a surface for furniture, walking, and gathering, and serving as a transition zone that pulls people from an indoor environment out to an outdoor environment.

From an aesthetic perspective, they help to define a space and give it character. By playing colors and textures against or with the architecture of structures, they can enhance the overall feelings created by the design. They can become a backdrop or they can provide a sense of midground or even foreground (see chapter 6, page 58). They also act as a textural contrast to the plastic horizontal plane of the lawn. In addition, they can help to create a greater sense of visual flow in the entire composition of the landscape.

Deck Choices

Decks are an increasingly popular item on many homes. This elevated wooden surface provides access to additional living space outside of the confines of the home. It is important that a deck is properly constructed in order to provide many years of service. We recommend using sonotubes filled with concrete for the supporting base. It is essential that there be good drainage around these foundation pourings and, if at all possible, that the foundation be below the frost line. The superstructure of the deck should be built of pressure-treated timbers.

Check to be sure this lumber is warranteed for at least forty years against rot.

Many varieties of wood may be used for finishing the actual deck surface, including red or white cedar, redwood, and cypress. You will want to check with a knowledgeable building contractor as to the best wood for use in your area. The best ones will have a high content of rot-resistant oils in them naturally. (Be careful not to use woods such as spruce and fir, as they have been proven not to have a long life when used in a deck.) There are many paints, water preservatives, and stains available to seal the wood and give the deck years of service and beauty. Before using one of these, you should again check with a professional familiar with local conditions and the pros and cons of using various stains versus paints.

When designing the deck, you will want to consider the different uses a deck can provide for your style of outdoor living. Many people find two or more levels to be both practical and aesthetically pleasing. You should also keep in mind the prominent landscape features around your house, such as streams, trees, and hills that your deck looks out upon. You must be careful in placing the railing on the deck so that it doesn't obstruct your view. Remember that a deck can be much more than a rectangle with a railing. Mimicking a river pattern or an architectural feature of your house — even building around a tree or incorporating a planter into a sitting area — can add beauty and interest. Occasionally people will add a trellis and other features that create shade over a portion of the deck.

Decks: Value Added

The value added by a deck is considerable. What was once an unused space can suddenly become the most popular center of activity for the family. If you entertain, it becomes a place for crowds of people to congregate and socialize (not to mention helping to cook the barbecue). It also can act as a transition zone between the house and other outdoor spaces (such as the patio, pool, or garden). The deck can also be a great place to incorporate a hot tub or a Jacuzzi into your home's features.

Arbor Design

A very popular way to create an outdoor passage or doorway is to use an arbor. This can be made of many different materials such as wood (cedar or redwood), stone, metal, plants (such as climbing vines or sheared evergreens), pipe, or brick. Arbors are wonderful support systems for vining plants such as grapes, wisteria, or clematis.

A typical arbor has four posts and serves as a portal from one area of the yard to another. It has strips of wood across the top, many times crisscrossed to support the vines and to create a roof of greenery. Some arbors have seats incorporated into the side walls.

Arbors: Value Added

The primary value of an arbor is that it helps to define distinct spaces in the yard. It can become a focal point in the pathway and creates a sense of mystery and intrigue for the curious visitor to the garden. This relatively inexpensive addition can make your landscape seem elegant and focused.

Use of Drip Edges and Drainages

When you're deciding whether or not to use gutters on your home, consider using drip edges as an alternative. When gutters are not used on a house, a drip line will form next to the foundation. The drip edge should be placed to contain this drip line. These areas are basically drainage ditches, lined with geotextile and filled with crushed stone. They're easy to maintain and effective in pulling water away from your foundation. We use crushed stone, weed barrier, and an edge that can be made out of brick, aluminum, or pressure-treated wood. The geotextile is important for two reasons: It helps to keep weeds out and to keep the surrounding soils from migrating into the crushed stone. Using drip edges in place of gutters virtually eliminates gutter cleaning (since there are no gutters other than over doors), thereby saving you time and money. Cleaning out leaves and painting wooden gutters are also eliminated. In northern climates, drip edges also eliminate ice build-up or ice dams, which can lead to water damage inside the house.

Drip edges can be used in place of gutters on your home, saving you money and the time involved in cleaning gutters. The edges are constructed by digging trenches adjacent to the house directly under the eaves. These should be lined with geotextile and filled with crushed stone.

A nice way to enhance the drip-edge areas is to top-dress them with a decorative stone. You can fill most of the trench with a less expensive stone and use river jack on top, for example, for a more decorative look.

Drip Edge: Value Added

The outward appearance of a drip edge also has functional value. Since the drip edge extends at least six inches beyond the end of the eaves, this creates a space that is two feet or more beyond the edge of the foundation. This means that plants have to be set out from the foundation. You should go at least another two feet from the outside border of the drip edge before planting any shrub. By doing this, you will have access to walls of your house; it will also allow greater air circulation. This helps not only the plants, but also the siding on your house.

A drip edge can be an aesthetic contribution to your home and landscape as well. In Japan, the drip edge is part of the landscape. Some beautiful examples of drip-edge design can be discovered by studying the foundations of Japanese homes and temples. Even the downspouts are special in some Japanese approaches.

They may be bells, funnels, or even chains that direct the water to a recession.

Choices in Lighting

Night landscape lighting can be very effective in adding dimension to your landscape. We recommend that you use low-voltage systems (12-volt DC), which you can add to a landscape at any time. This will eliminate almost any possibility of electrical injury. This is because a 12-volt system uses a transformer, changing your 120 household current to voltage that's only a few volts higher than that of your telephone. Many companies now make extensive lines of beautiful outdoor fixtures.

Consider "up lighting" that special ornamental tree, or using diffused lighting to create soft shadows or to illuminate a path. Even security lighting can be attractive and effective. If you're building a new home, providing outdoor plugs and hard wiring (120 voltage house current) for spotlights is very helpful for immediate lighting or adding Christmas or other seasonal lights. The plugs will also be helpful if 12-volt lighting is added later. Whatever your preference,

Lighting performs a variety of purposes in the landscape: Down lighting (A) spotlights areas and produces interesting shadows; up lighting (B) can be used to highlight an ornamental tree or produce diffused light; security lighting (C) helps to illuminate entryways.

lighting done with taste and care can add value and interest to any landscape. There are many uses for outdoor lighting. Here are some of the more popular ones:

- **Down Lighting:** Lighting an area or object from above is down lighting. It is an effective way to create interesting shadows, while helping to spotlight an area.
- **Security Lighting:** Property-protection and entrance illumination are useful as both insurance against intruders and safe passage.
- **Up Lighting:** Lighting objects from below.
- **Diffused Lighting:** Using a light source behind a translucent object. It is considered to be a passive form of light.
- **Moonlighting:** Using small lights placed above objects to cast a soft light and create an ambience of distant moonlight on a focal point. Very attractive!
- **Area Lighting:** Use this method to illuminate a patio or deck for entertaining.
- **Accent Lighting:** We use this method to draw attention to a particular plant in a garden or perhaps to a statue. This is a very effective technique to add zip to your nighttime landscape.

For landscape lighting, we recommend that you use household current for your major spotlights and 12-volt systems for everything else. The 12-volt system is much cheaper to run and the new lines are far more versatile than 120 systems. To determine the brightness of the light, refer to the number of watts a bulb will consume during use. This information is usually found on the box or printed right on the bulb.

There are four major types of lightbulbs or lamps:

- **Incandescent lamps** (lightbulbs) are the most commonly used. They use a glowing tungsten thread filament within a glass globe to produce light. The standard "A"

type bulb is most commonly used indoors. Other bulb types in this category are "R" (reflector) type, "ER" (elliptical reflector) type, and "PAR" (parabolic aluminized reflector) type. These lamps are frequently used in low-voltage systems.
- **Quartz incandescent lamps** give a constant bright light. They use the same working principles as the straight incandescent lamp.
- **Fluorescent lamps** use a phosphor coating inside a glass tube excited by an electrical current to create light.
- **High-intensity discharge lamps, mercury vapor, high-pressure sodium, and halide lamps** are pressurized bulbs that use gases excited by the electrical current to produce light.

Typical outdoor lighting uses incandescent types of lamps. Most low-voltage lighting is in this category as well.

Lighting: Value Added

The practical value of lighting for safety and security is quite evident. So also is the function of making a space usable in the evening that would otherwise be accessible only in daylight hours.

The attributes of landscape lighting from an aesthetic perspective are more subtle but may actually outstrip the enormous practical value. You can create focal points that would not be noticeable in the daytime. You can create moods and feelings by controlling the levels of lighting. For example, "electric eyes" and computers combined with rheostats can create some very dramatic effects for someone entering into a space. An electric eye can turn on the lighting as you walk through the landscape, while colors can be blended and modified with light to create a mood, and to enhance and vary the sense of depth.

Selecting Fencing

When many of us think of fences, a few commonly used types come to mind, such as picket, split rail, and stockade. Brick or concrete fences can be used to create courtyards and hidden gardens or to surround estates. Fences are also frequently used as screening, to hide the view of a neighbor, highway, or something else you don't want to see. When you're considering using a fence, be sure to explore all of the possible materials, and to think about the fence's location and purpose. A well-placed fence, creatively designed and conceived, can add tremendously to the perceived value of your landscape.

Four Functions of Fencing

1

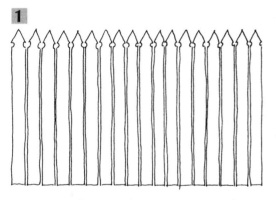

Screening fences *obstruct unwanted views.*

3

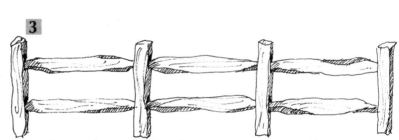

Perimeter fences *define the property or a specific area.*

2

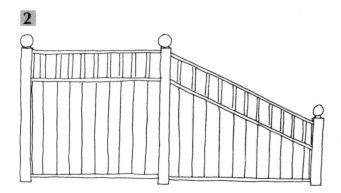

Sleeve fences *(term inspired by the Japanese kimono sleeve) are an attractive way to hide an unwanted view and define the area in front of it.*

4

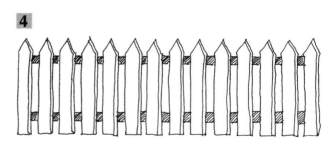

Accent fences *draw attention to an attractive or interesting part of the landscape.*

Wood and metal are most often used in fence construction. Less common materials are bamboo, plastic, canvas, and even living plants such as hornbeam, apple, cherry, arborvitae, and willow. When using living materials, we recommend that you consider a diverse number of plant varieties that could suit your situation. One interesting style of living fence is called "espalier." Fruit trees are often used for this type of pruning, but anything that is upright and can be pruned into a two-dimensional plant can work. Different patterns are formed with the growing branches, and they will often be grafted to each other.

An espalier or "living fence" is an attractive alternative to traditional fencing.

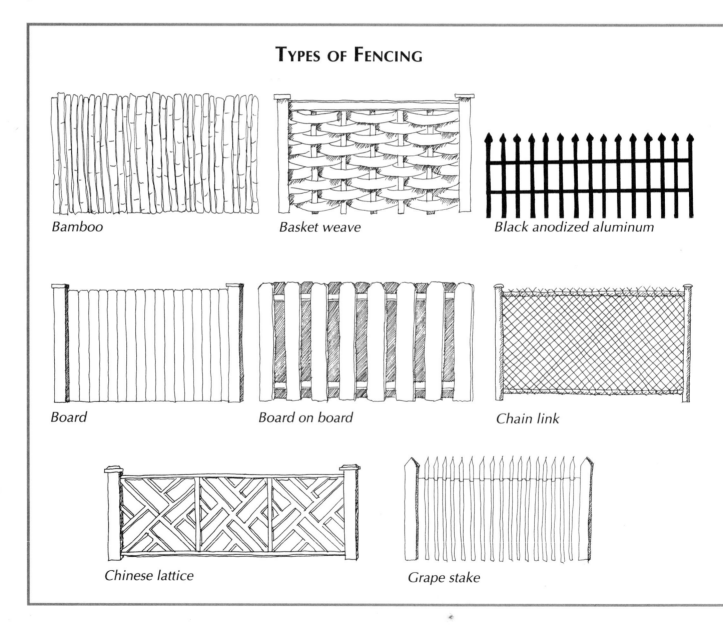

TYPES OF FENCING

Bamboo

Basket weave

Black anodized aluminum

Board

Board on board

Chain link

Chinese lattice

Grape stake

Fencing: Value Added

Fences contribute to value because they provide containment, privacy, and support. Many people value privacy. They enjoy the escape from the stresses of public life and relish slipping into their own private little world. In the city, privacy fences are almost essential for a plot of land. Containment fences provide an opportunity to keep animals or children safe from exposure to the outside world, or vice versa. In general, fewer people need this function compared to people looking for privacy. Support fences, such as lattice and trellis, generally provide the least amount of value, since their application is limited and seasonal.

Aesthetically, fences help to define a space and add character to that space. They are also effective in helping to create a sense of depth in the landscape. A fence in context with the architecture or theme of the landscape will unify the entire picture or tableau of the property. Fences also can help to stop the eye and to lead the eye to other parts of the garden. Traditional uses of fences, such as in a courtyard entry garden, can be a connection to a cultural or regional heritage — a pull to the heartstrings of the buyer looking at your home.

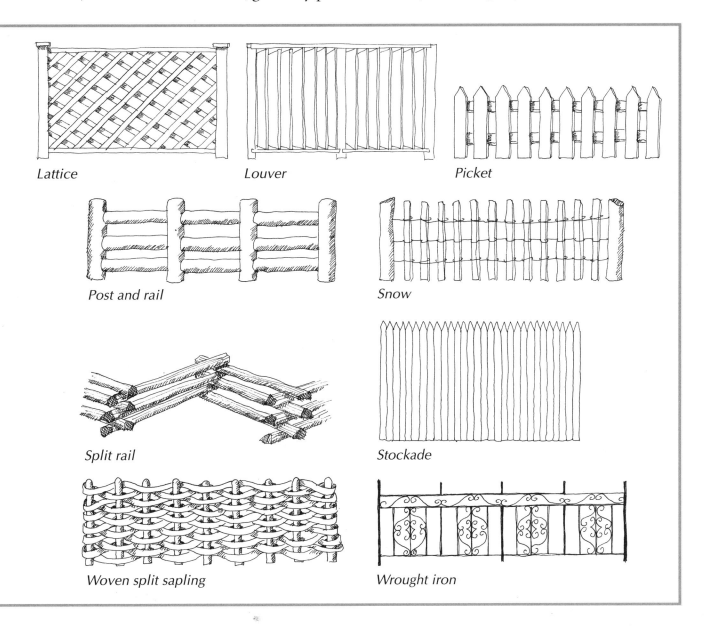

Lattice

Louver

Picket

Post and rail

Snow

Split rail

Stockade

Woven split sapling

Wrought iron

Options in Water Gardens

The use of water in the landscape has recently opened new dimensions in the yard. Some landscape professionals, realizing the potential of water gardens, have devoted their entire businesses to this field. Water in the landscape can have a very powerful influence on people's feelings and can establish the yard's entire mood. It provides new ways for the senses to enjoy the garden — the sound of water and its cooling touch add another dimension to the visual effect. Water can reflect the world around us, creating the feeling of a larger garden.

Water gardens fall into two major groups: formal and informal. The formal style, the usual choice for the gardens of the western world, is symmetrical. If you were to divide a formal pool in half, each side might be a mirror image of the other.

Informal water features are an integral part of Asian gardens. Inspiration for these gardens comes from nature. Some of their features are waterfalls, reflecting pools, fountains, and streams. The need to use water in Asian-influenced gardens is so strong that in the absence of water, other mediums such as pebbles or gravel are often used, to mimic water and the effects of water. The use of water can also be implied by the placing of objects into the landscape that could convey water: typically wells, water troughs, and aqueducts.

We have found that there are many other reasons to add water to your landscape. If you have a traffic noise problem, for example, the use of moving water can help to mask the offensive sounds. The sound of water also creates a serene feeling that helps to soothe nerves frayed by a high-stress world. (Dentists sometimes use a sound similar to the sound of moving water, called "white noise," that can actually help calm people and block pain messages.)

Water gardens also provide a habitat for fish and other aquatic plant and animal life. Children absolutely love water life. A pool designed with your children's use in mind can be invaluable as a teaching tool, particularly in urban areas. Of course you want to be sure that the pool is shallow and would not pose a safety hazard to small children. Children should always be supervised around water.

The main types of garden pools are clay lined, molded, free-form lined, and dammed, in addition to those that occur naturally. We have found that the installation is not difficult for smaller pools, if you consider a couple of site features. Be sure to pick a site where the plants and fish will receive five or more hours of sunlight a day. Also, avoid sites with heavy leaf fall.

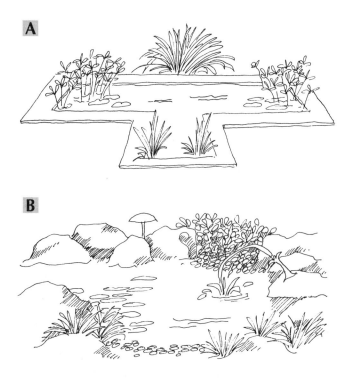

Water gardens can be constructed symmetrically for a formal look (A) or more naturally for an informal look (B).

Installation Tips

A garden pool can be installed by following the manufacturer's recommendations. When digging, consider the following: Call your power company if you have concerns about power, cable, telephone, or gas lines in the area that you are digging, or the "Dig Safe" 800 number for your state (this service will locate all underground utilities on your property). Don't place your pool in any low spots that attract large amounts of runoff, to avoid silt and debris filling your pool every time it rains. The subsoils will help you to determine how much drainage will be necessary under the pool. The same rules that apply to walls and patios apply here: If the soils are silty clay types that don't percolate water well, you must have a more elaborate drainage system.

A cushion of sand is a good idea when you have chosen a vinyl rolled liner for your pool. Fiberglass pool liners in northern climates need good drainage or the whole structure can pop out of the ground when water trapped underneath it freezes and expands in the winter. One common problem of water gardens is algal buildup. The use of pumps and filters helps to control the algae. There are also some mild chemicals safe to use with fish to help in alga control. Another control is alga-eating fish or snails. Another common but controllable problem is evaporation. Water evaporation can be controlled by the use of large-leaved water plants growing in the pool and plants placed

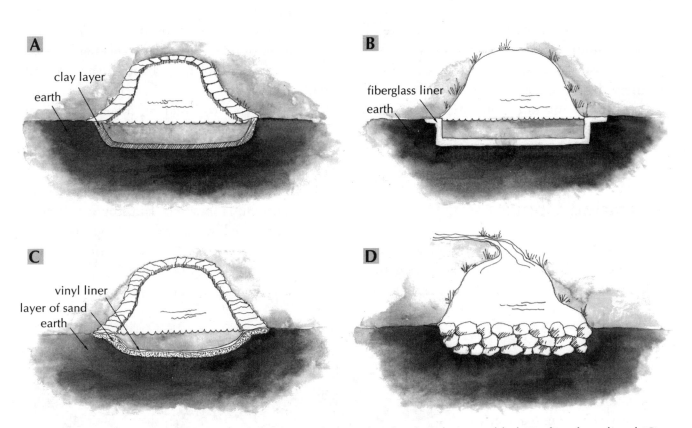

There are four primary ways of constructing garden pools: clay-lined (A), molded (B), free-form lined (C), and dammed (D).

around the rim. These plants can help to reduce the water surface directly exposed to the sun's heat.

Water Gardens: Value Added

The value provided by water gardens tends to be emotional and is difficult to quantify. The practical aspects of sound abatement are one element, but more significant are the feelings created by staring into water or a descending path of a waterfall. It seems to touch a part of the psyche and answers some basic need we all have.

Irrigation Choices

Watering your plants in the landscape is of paramount importance. Underground irrigation systems are engineered to be low maintenance and efficient, and could save you the loss of expensive plants from lack of water. New technology has made these systems excellent insurance against drought and neglect. This is particularly true in areas without reliable rainfall.

Another exciting innovation in irrigation is the advent of the pipe-puller, a mechanical system that can pull pipes through the ground without trenching or digging. This tool allows the homeowner to install an irrigation system with minimum expense and disruption. This means that it's never too late for the installation. However, if you're building a new house, it's advisable to plan on installation of irrigation during the initial phase of landscaping. Irrigation can be used to water everything from vegetables to grass, flowers to foundation shrubs. New systems are made of durable plastic and metals. Remember, a plant that is watered correctly will grow!

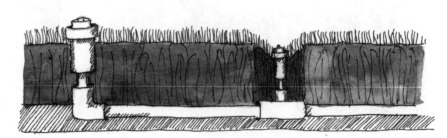

An underground irrigation system can protect against the loss of expensive plantings that may otherwise be subject to the effects of drought or neglect.

Irrigation Systems: Value Added

The primary value derived from an irrigation system is the maintenance of the planted material in the landscape. However, a movement currently afoot in the landscape industry downplays the installation of irrigation systems because of water shortages in many parts of the country. As water becomes a more precious commodity, its use for landscape plants may not be the highest priority. Environmentally sensitive landscape designers and architects are supplementing their planting palettes with plants that are far more drought tolerant.

Poor installation of irrigation systems can sever the roots of established trees. Irrigation used in poorly drained soil can also lead to rotting tree roots. The tree responds to the excess of water by growing a beautiful, thick head of leaves and looks as healthy as can be. However, such a tree may topple in a windstorm because the roots have rotted away.

Saturation-based irrigation systems store water in underground cisterns activated by "smart pumps" only when conditions warrant. They are relatively expensive, but in the long term they will pay for themselves.

The bottom line for the value of irrigation: It depends. Consider your area and determine if irrigation is the right choice for you and your landscape. It would be helpful to get the opinion of a professional who does not have a personal interest in selling you irrigation.

Types of Raised Plant Beds

Raised plant beds can add linear form and depth to the yard. Many people like to put herbs in these raised plant beds. One of their advantages is that you can get away with an earlier planting time. These beds will drain water off quickly, making planting of cold-weather-tolerant plants easier in northern climates.

Raised beds or terraced areas are an excellent approach for a hill or slope. These beds are frequently made of stone or wood. Pressure-treated wood has become popular as a less expensive and long-lived alternative to cedar or redwood. As with all structures, the drainage and method of construction are crucial to their success and integrity.

Stone planters should always have a batter and be lined with geotextile. Wood retaining

In building a raised bed into a hillside, "deadman" timbers running perpendicular to the front wall helps to keep it plumb.

A sloped area of your yard is a good location to add a raised bed built from stone.

or terraced structures should always have cribbing or "deadman" construction. (See the Glossary for more information on these types of construction.) It is also important that loam be deep enough to support robust plant life.

Raised Beds: Value Added

In addition to the early planting afforded by a raised bed, you also gain some value by creating vertical relief in the landscape. This can also be accomplished with a berm. A berm is basically a raised bed without the benefit of supports on the sides. This can create mystery and a sense of discovery if used effectively in the landscape design.

Choices in Yard and Garden Structures

Landscape planning often overlooks the "out" buildings. These structures are most often made from wood, but masonry of various kinds is frequently used as well. There are many choices of wood for use outside. We recommend that you talk to your local lumberyard to determine what's best for your budget.

Pool Shed

If you're planning a swimming pool, you should also plan a place for people to change and take a shower. It's best to consider an outside shower attached to a pool shed. It can become a real housekeeping nightmare to have people tracking water and dirt through the house to shower.

Try to tailor the "out" buildings on your property to fit the activities you plan to host there. For instance, a swimming pool is greatly enhanced by a pool shed where people can change their clothes.

Tips for Working with Timber

Buying timber. When buying any type of timber, check each piece to make sure it is not warped. When buying pressure-treated timber, be sure that you are getting timbers that have a guarantee. A forty-year warranty is not uncommon.

Working with timber. When storing timbers, stack them up off the ground in a dry location. When cutting pressure-treated timbers, use a chain saw or ripsaw. Always use appropriate safety gear for the task you are performing. This means helmets, eye protection, hearing protection, gloves, and using a respirator when you create a fine dust, such as when cutting pressure-treated wood. Use a paper match to remove foreign particles from your eyes, and keep a bucket or bowl of water handy for flushing out your eyes when using caustic materials such as acids and wood preservatives. Use ten- or twelve-inch spikes when using five- or six-inch timbers. Drill pilot holes in the timbers before spiking together; countersink spikes and cover the holes with a piece of dowel.

Storage Shed

You may want to consider a storage shed with an overhang for drying firewood. Keep in mind that the opening on the overhang should face south. You'll need to provide space behind the stacked wood to facilitate air flow. This shed also can be a convenient place to create a potting area, with a cold frame or greenhouse attached.

If your home includes a wood-burning stove, a wood-storage shed can be a great asset to your property. It can double as a greenhouse.

Playhouse

Folks with families often install playhouses and treehouses for their children, and in some landscapes create whole areas devoted to their children's entertainment, such as sandboxes, swing sets, and jungle gyms, as well as basketball and volleyball courts. When children are asked to take an active role in the design of the landscape, wonderfully fresh ideas emerge. There is some concern over the use of pressure-treated wood for structures where children play, since exposure to the wood preservatives can be hazardous. Check with your professional contractor.

Gazebo, Ramada, Shade House

Additional out-structures are also occasionally used in the landscape. The most common of these is a gazebo. These first gained popularity during the Victorian era, and can often be found as part of the landscape of a Victorian-style home. These were popular because they provided shelter within the garden itself. They

A shade house offers shelter from the sun and a great place for plants.

A gazebo makes a nice gathering place in your garden or yard.

were basically octagonal in shape, with large openings along each of the sides for an unobstructed view of the beautiful surrounding garden. A ramada is an open shelter, often having a thatched roof in a dome shape, and is usually found in picnic areas or on beaches. They lend the feeling of the tropics to a landscape. Shade houses, on the other hand, are usually rectangular, with a roof consisting of lattice or lathing strips to break up the sunlight. The spacing and width of the strips or lathing determine the degree of shade provided.

Yard and Garden Structures: Value Added

The value of all structures is largely based on the quality of the construction, the continued maintenance, and the overall appeal and usability of the structure itself. A well-built gazebo that overlooks a beautiful scene, has an attractive path leading to it, and "beckons" you to visit is likely to have considerable value. If it's rundown, hidden, and looks out on a pile of debris, it has done little to add value — and may, in fact, reduce value.

Other Miscellaneous Hardscaping Options

Numerous items are also very important to the overall feeling of the landscape. These items are like the seasonings that are added to a good stew to make it great.

Flagpoles

Flagpoles for flying our nation's colors are often used by people to show their patriotic feelings. The poles and flags also can suggest a nautical theme with the use of old masts or spars.

Sculpture

Sculpture in the landscape can add just the right accent. As you consider the use of sculpture in different parts of the yard, you will begin to comprehend the wide array of items that fall into this category. Sculpture ranges from carved stone to garden gnomes, as well as pink flamingos, mobiles, wind chimes, or bronze statuary. Accent stone or boulders could be considered sculpture as well.

Birdhouses and Feeders

Birds are an integral part of any landscape. You can encourage birds by offering them houses and feeders. Many people have discovered the benefits of having martin or swallow houses — these birds eat hundreds of insects a day. Birdbaths will also attract certain varieties of birds, and can be interesting additions of functional sculpture when made from granite or concrete. Bats also have been added recently to the picture of the complete yard. If you can get over the stigma attached to bats, you'll find that they are the best form of natural mosquito control. Bat houses and "condos" will attract these mosquito catchers to your yard.

Benches

Benches have a place in all landscapes. They are components of the yard that ask you to come out, sit down, and enjoy the fruits of your labor. They can be made from wood, stone, or metal. They can be as ornate and formal as a polished marble bench or as informal as a log sitting on the ground. Hammocks also have that "come-out-and-enjoy-the-yard" quality. Even if you don't use yours very frequently, just knowing it is there can be soothing!

Mailboxes

Mailboxes also have been added to the list, as well as the posts used to hold them. Many companies offer a variety of painted designs, such as birds, flowers, and evergreen motifs. The posts are made from granite and wrought iron, and also may take on a regional theme (in the Florida Keys, you will see concrete manatees holding mailboxes).

Miscellaneous Items

A couple of other items for finishing off the yard with personal touches are sundials and planter pots. Pots can be as simple as smooth red clay or be as complex as a granite pot with Greek Revivalist art carved on it. The ability to move the plants around from year to year is very appealing to some.

Other Options: Value Added

There are many elements to the hardscape, as this chapter demonstrates. Each of them has an important role to play in your yard. Remember that the correct installation methods are not always going to be the least expensive up front, but in the long run could save you costly repairs.

The hardscape elements also add a sense of stability and permanence to the yard that adds peace of mind and considerable value. Because brick and stone are so much a part of our common heritage, when you look at a stone wall or meandering brick walk that trails away through a garden and to parts unknown, a sense of connection to our country's history envelops you. The backbone of a landscape is the hardscape — remember to make it part of your yard and garden.

Hardscaping elements offer a way to personalize your landscape and make it feel like home.

8

Investing in Softscaping Elements

~

IN THIS CHAPTER, WE HOPE TO MAKE YOU FEEL more comfortable with an understanding of the terms used in landscaping and to give you a better idea of the range of options available to you. There is always more to know, and we recommend that you accumulate a good library of reference books. The section "For Further Reading" at the end of this book will give you a list of titles. Each of the plant types briefly mentioned here is the subject of many different books. It is best to browse through here and see what strikes your fancy and then begin a journey to becoming a better-informed gardener. If this does not interest you, you can at least be able to hold an intelligent conversation with your contractor and be better informed about options that you should or should not be considering.

The term *softscaping* is applied to the growing elements of the landscape, and to the practices that encourage their growth. It is a complex field that is primarily associated with horticulture, and is called "soft" scaping because most of the elements used are just that — soft.

To pull the various elements together in a way that is pleasing to the eye and nurturing to the plants is quite challenging. It can be compared with putting together a jigsaw puzzle. If you simply tumble the pieces of the puzzle onto a table, it's not very attractive, and doesn't provide you with the picture you want to see. But once you start putting the pieces together, the scene begins to emerge, and the picture becomes easier to complete. It's important to keep your list of priorities in mind (see chapter 6) when looking at all the variables as you decide what you'll use and where you'll be putting it.

When deciding what types of plants to use, you need to understand the basic range of options

Softscaping *refers to all the living, growing elements of the landscape including trees, shrubs, flowers, and ground covers. Making softscaping choices is an exciting and challenging part of landscaping.*

available. The world of plants is diverse and their application in our landscape knows no bounds. Don't be content to deal with only a few types of plants. Experiment and explore the worlds of beauty that you can create with this cornucopia of choices. Remember that the choices you make should be guided by experience and knowledge of the results you can expect. This knowledge is best gained by talking directly to your landscape or nursery professional.

In this chapter, we examine the major categories of plants. Deciduous trees are discussed in the major heading of "Trees," as are evergreen and broad-leaved evergreen trees. Within these categories, we consider the contributions each group makes to the landscape as well as some factors to consider for placement and installation. Refer to chapter 12 for specific questions and concerns about these major groupings.

This information applies whether you are having the work contracted or you are doing the planting yourself.

Choices in Trees

Trees are the ruling monarchs of the softscape. Upright and stately, with spreading canopies, they can truly dominate the landscape. From a design perspective they serve two primary purposes: *functional* — such as providing fruit, shade, or breeze; and *aesthetic* — such as introducing varying bark and leaf textures, thrusting vertical framing elements, or potentially angular, distorted forms into the landscape.

Evergreen trees are usually the most effective year-round screening, whereas deciduous trees provide a number of other less tangible benefits, such as solar heating for passive solar homes in the winter and shade in the summer. There are a few oddball trees out there that don't fit into a neat category, and you may not immediately recognize them. For instance, some typical "deciduous conifers" would be bald cypress, dawn redwood, and larch. Although they have needles and bear cones, they are also deciduous because they lose the needles in the fall of the year.

When buying trees in a nursery or garden center, you'll find plants available in a variety of different ways: bareroot; plastic, metal, and wooden containers; balled and burlapped; balled with plastic burlap; and the most dreaded of all, the plastic bag.

Trees: Value Added

Trees are one of the most valuable types of plant you can put in your yard. They provide one of the quickest returns on money spent,

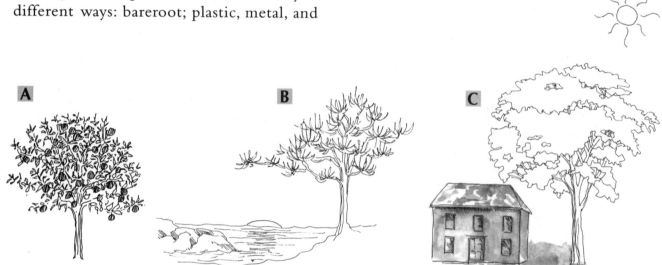

Trees serve a variety of purposes in the landscape, such as bearing fruit (A), introducing aesthetic contrast to or helping to frame other elements in the landscape (B), and offering shade (C).

Tips for Installing Softscaping

In this chapter, you will learn some of our best techniques for landscape-planting installation as well as some money- and time-saving tips. Although this chapter is aimed more at the do-it-yourselfer, it is not a comprehensive how-to manual. (We do recommend some of those in the "For Further Reading" section at the back of the book.)

We suggest that you use this chapter for information about the correct methods for many of the procedures for installing plants, either for yourself or for understanding the work that someone is doing for you. For example, take planting trees. Many different methods are employed in the industry today. These tips will help you to know when the procedures you see being used in your installation are correct or if they need to be challenged.

We are not stating that our methods are appropriate in all circumstances! Reputable landscape contractors devise various techniques that are effective and correct for their region of the country. A good contractor will be able to defend these practices based on experience. We want you to have confidence in the work performed on your property and to know that you are getting good value for your landscape dollar. If you are doing the work yourself, and you do not have the benefit of a contractor's experience, you may want to augment this chapter with a good how-to book on landscape installation for your region.

especially if they're properly maintained. They also provide a significant long-term investment because the physical size plays an important role in their value. The fine tuning of this investment lies in the proper placement of the plant in your landscape. Keep in mind some of the various functions provided by the plant: shade in the summer (reduced cooling costs), better air quality (reduced health care), sun in the winter (reduced heating costs), fruit production (reduced food costs), and noise buffer (reduced stress).

Types of Shrubs

Shrubs, like trees, play an important role in the complete landscape. We recommend that you thoroughly explore this diverse arena of expression. Purchase a good shrub book and visit your local garden center.

Another way to become acquainted with shrubs is to visit an arboretum. Here you can see shrubs and trees that are fully grown. Just seeing these shrubs in their mature state will

BASIC TYPES OF PLANTS AND TREES

Alpine Plants
Annuals
Biennials
Bog Plants
Broad-Leaved Evergreen Shrubs
Broad-Leaved Evergreen Trees
Bulbs, Corms, Tubers
Cacti
Deciduous Shrubs
Deciduous Trees
Deciduous Vines
Evergreen Shrubs
Evergreen Trees
Evergreen Vines
Ferns, Mosses, Liverworts, Lycopodiums
Ground Covers
Herbs
Lawn Grasses
Open-Water Plants
Ornamental Grasses
Perennials
Roses
Vegetables
Wildflowers and Woodland Plants

Tips for Planting

Take great care when moving and handling your plant. It's easy at this point (particularly when you're making those final placement adjustments) to break the dirt away from the roots with rough treatment — so don't. Remember, your plant's rootball must not be dropped from the back of a truck or dumped off a wheelbarrow. Make sure you have enough help to lift the plant easily. Also, never lift a plant by grabbing it by the stem. Always lift from the base. It is sometimes helpful to have help lifting the crown (the top of the plant), particularly for a large tree or shrub. If your plant is too heavy to be lifted manually, we recommend that you hire a qualified professional with equipment for lifting and planting correctly.

help with the concepts of design and companion planting. We recommend a visit to an arboretum as a fun family excursion, especially for anyone doing landscaping.

As a design element, shrubs are used as focal points, or as massed plantings. They are also useful as screens, hedges, and food sources for birds and other wildlife. The growth habits of shrubs are extensive and range from tall (treelike) to low and prostrate. You can use evergreens for year-round interest, providing a wide array of colors and textures. Deciduous and broad-leaved evergreen plants exhibit numerous flowering cycles and growth forms and can provide continual bloom in the landscape.

Like trees, shrubs come from the nursery in a variety of packaging: bareroot; plastic, metal, or wooden containers; balled and burlapped; balled with plastic burlap; and again, the dreaded plastic bag.

Shrubs: Value Added

The value of shrubs is apparent when you explore their versatility and variety. Different shrubs bloom at all times of the year. In order to maximize the value of the plant, it is extremely important to look at the growth form and habit. One of the biggest mistakes is to use the wrong plant in the wrong location. By way of example, let's look at yews. This is a commonly used (pardon the pun) foundation plant in the northeast and central United States. People seem to think that a yew is a yew is a yew. Nothing could be farther from the truth. If you look closely at the way the new growth comes out of the plant, you'll be given a clue about the plant's eventual form. If a stem grows out one inch for every four inches it grows up, the mature plant is likely to have a shape that follows that same ratio. A mistake people often make is to plant a yew that's going to grow tall and narrow, and then to try to shear it so that it grows into a cube, or to have a yew that wants

TYPES OF YEW PLANTS

Type	Growth Pattern
A. Hicksii Yew	Narrow and upright
B. Hatfield Yew	Broad and upright
C. Brownii Yew	Globe
D. Wardii Yew	Low and flat
E. Robusta Yew	Very narrow and upright
F. Spreading Yew	Broad and spreading

to grow into a cube and try to make it tall and narrow.

Remember — to get the right plant in the right place, you must look at the growth form when considering its placement. The best way to do this is to consult with a professional nurseryperson or landscape professional before planting.

Choices in Vining Plants

A special consideration with vines is their unique growth form. They can grow on arbors, fences, and buildings. They can be used for fruit production, creation of shade, screening, and the softening of architectural elements. When used on a building, the vines have to be compatible with the building material. The two basic growth forms are twining and holdfasts. With twining, the vine needs to have a trellis to support its growth, or hooks embedded into a masonry surface. The holdfasts actually cling to the surface they're growing on. The problem with this form of growth is that it makes maintenance of the surface (painting of wood or repointing of bricks) impossible and requires the entire removal of the vine. This is not the end of the world, however, because the plant usually has a well-established root system and will grow back quickly.

Vining Plants: Value Added

One of the greatest values of vines is the way they can modify the feeling of a space. The cool shade produced by a grape arbor or wisteria on a pergola can offer a dramatic contrast to a hot, sultry day in the sun. Vines such as grapes, bittersweet, honeysuckle, and trumpet creeper can also attract wildlife, since they are important sources of food for various animals, including people. Seasonal color through flowers or fall foliage can also be appealing. Environmental contributions of vines can also be significant in terms of their cooling capabilities — a vine covering the south side of a building can reduce the demand on air-conditioning.

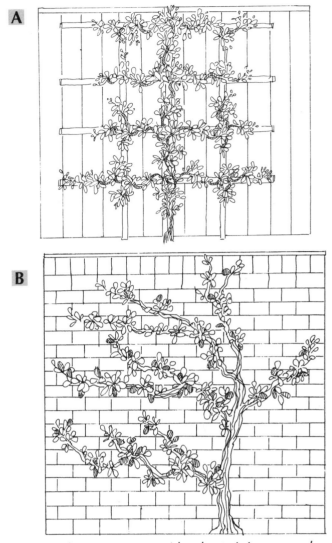

Vining plants may grow either by twining around a trellis or other support (A), or as holdfast plants that cling directly to the wall or surface they're growing on (B).

Rose Selections

Throughout history, the rose and other members of its family have played important ornamental and agricultural roles. The genus of *Rosa* has a variety of forms and bloom cycles, and many are fragrant in addition to being beautiful. Here are some of the varieties that you may wish to include: hybrid tea, grandiflora, floribunda, shrub, rugosa, wichuraiana, centifolia, damask, gallica, climbers, and miniature roses.

Other plants that are not commonly known as members of the rose family are apples, cherries, peaches, pears, raspberries, blackberries, and flowering shad, as well as a number of ornamental shrubs, including the spireas.

Some varieties and forms of roses are considered to be very high-maintenance plants, and we don't recommend these to the novice gardener. Everyone, however, can grow shrub, rugosa, and climbing roses with relative ease — consider them for your landscape. Give them plenty of sun, good drainage, and good air circulation, and be prepared for pest problems. Roses are particularly susceptible to damage from insects and diseases. Rose chafers and Japanese beetles are two of the most common culprits, and you should study up on the life cycles of these pests in your area so that you can combat them.

Roses: Value Added

Roses are a passion and obsession for some people. Rose enthusiasts will arrange their entire lives around their rose gardens. For the majority of gardeners, however, growing roses is not a challenge as much as it is a frustration. The amount of care required by a rose garden makes it questionable as a value-added element to the landscape — except when you have a beautiful garden in full bloom at the time that you are selling the property. Cut roses in vases in the home can also create a feeling of elegance.

Roses add beauty to the landscape whether you grow a shrub, rugosa, or climbing variety.

Choices in Herbaceous Plants

This group of plants, which include perennials, annuals, biennials, and ornamental grasses, is very popular, and brings to the garden a variety of colors, textures, and forms. They are usually seasonal, and require more maintenance than shrubs and trees. Many forms spread by underground runners, and others develop as a central clump of vegetation.

This group of plants is sold at the garden center in a variety of ways: bareroot, or in peat pots, plastic pots, cell pacs, containers, or nursery or garden flats.

Herbaceous Plants: Value Added

Few people can deny the beauty of a flower garden, an English cottage garden, or a wild-flower meadow. The brilliant palette of colors they offer and artistic blending of the various hues and textures of these plants make them a noteworthy addition to any garden.

As a design element, these plants can become a unifying element within the landscape, especially when used in the form of a ground cover. Low-growing ground plants, en masse, become a substitute for bark mulch and reduce the need for mulch replacement, not to mention weeding. Another common use is accent plants or bedding plants for seasonal color or texture. In order to maintain value, it is essential that you provide continual maintenance for this type of planting. We recommend that you pay close attention to the plants considered to be low maintenance, and that you start small with this type of garden, so that you know what you'll be dealing with.

Insect and Disease Control

Literally hundreds of insects and diseases can damage your plants. You can deal with these problems in three ways: organic pest control, chemical pest control, and companion planting. You can combine some or all of these to get the best results. Most of the non-chemical approaches are the easiest and least expensive and, in the long run, have no detrimental effects on your property or its value. By choosing your plants wisely, you can work with varieties that are naturally resistant to many of the common pests (see the "For Further Reading" section at the back of the book).

The most common plant diseases are fungal and can be very difficult to control once they're established. It's best to deal with this through prevention. Provide the plant with the correct growing conditions — proper light, air circulation, and moisture. If you decide to use a fungicide or an insecticide, we strongly recommend that you carefully read each container's instructions about application and storage. We also recommend you dispose of any leftover material and the containers safely — the best idea is to return the containers to the nursery they came from.

> ## OUTLINE OF PERENNIAL MAINTENANCE TASKS
>
> **Spring**
> 1. Rake off top layer of mulch
> 2. Clip off and clean up dead stalks
> 3. Divide root stalk as necessary
> 4. Remove evident weeds
> 5. Plant summer- and fall-blooming bulbs
> 6. Add new plants to the garden
> 7. Top-dress mulch (do not exceed 2" total)
>
> **Summer**
> 1. Fertilize in early summer
> 2. Irrigate
> 3. Staking
> 4. Pinching or debudding
> 5. Deadheading
> 6. Weeding
> 7. Pest and disease control
> 8. Cutting and enjoying
>
> **Autumn**
> 1. Division
> 2. Cleanup
> 3. Cutback
> 4. Mulching
> 5. Liming (if necessary)
>
> **Winter**
> 1. Perusing garden catalogs
> 2. Ordering from garden catalogs
>   (see the section "For Further Reading" for books about growing perennials)

A perennial flower bed is a major source of color and texture in any landscape.

Tips for Maintaining Herbaceous Plants

Here are a few guidelines for keeping your plants healthy and vigorous for many years to come:

Checking the soil's pH. Compare your soil's pH to the needs of the plants you're installing. Some plants are very particular in their needs and others could care less, or are at least very flexible. Garden centers and hardware stores often sell pH-testing kits for the homeowner who wants immediate feedback. A more detailed test is available through your local university or Cooperative Extension Service.

Digging a perennial bed. Double-dig to ensure that your plants have the appropriate type and amount of soil. Since most herbaceous plants are established in planting beds, double-digging is fairly easy to do. Begin by digging out the top twelve inches of soil and putting it in a pile. Then dig out the next twelve inches and place it in a separate pile. Next, with soil from the first pile, begin to fill in the hole that you've created. Necessary amendments, such as peat, lime, sulfur, manure, or gypsum, can be mixed into the remaining pile of soil at this time.

When you run out of soil from the first pile, continue to fill the bed with the amended soil from the second pile. This process gives your plants, whatever they may be, an excellent medium where they can get established. It also provides good drainage and reduces the quantity of weeds.

Planting holes should be wide but not deep. The depth of the hole should be the same as the depth of the root mass.

Fertilizing. The pH of the soil will also help determine how you fertilize. Fertilizing is more than just throwing some manure around the base of the plant to make it grow bigger. It is a complex dynamic that is affected by relative moisture in the soil, the pH of the soil, soil structure, the specific needs of the plant, and many other variables. For example, the relative acidity can play a large part in determining what plants will thrive in an environment regardless of the amount of fertilizing. If the pH is not correct, the plant can't absorb the nutrients provided by fertilizing.

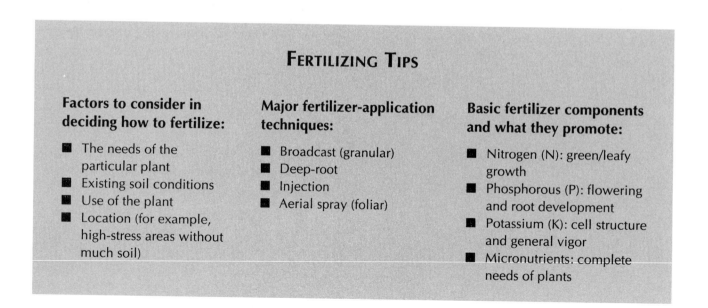

FERTILIZING TIPS

Factors to consider in deciding how to fertilize:

- The needs of the particular plant
- Existing soil conditions
- Use of the plant
- Location (for example, high-stress areas without much soil)

Major fertilizer-application techniques:

- Broadcast (granular)
- Deep-root
- Injection
- Aerial spray (foliar)

Basic fertilizer components and what they promote:

- Nitrogen (N): green/leafy growth
- Phosphorous (P): flowering and root development
- Potassium (K): cell structure and general vigor
- Micronutrients: complete needs of plants

Watering. We've said this many times, but it bears repeating: Water is the "poor man's fertilizer," and is the lifeblood of the plant. Be sure your flowers receive adequate amounts, but be careful not to overwater. Unfortunately, most of the indicators of overwatering are similar to those of drought: drooping leaves, yellow leaf margins, leaf drop. You can purchase a moisture meter that has a metal probe that goes into the soil and a dial that shows when the soil is too wet or dry.

Pruning. Pruning this type of plant is usually seasonal and consists of deadheading (the removal of faded, spent flowers), pinching and debudding (resulting in a more compact and floriferous plant), stalk removal (usually done in the fall or spring, depending on personal preference), and summer cutback (which is done to promote a second blooming).

Note: Stalks of some perennials need to be removed in the fall. Check with a qualified nursery professional for further guidance.

Dividing. Dividing perennials that are overcrowded, or that you want to use in other places in the garden, generally can be done at any time from spring to fall. (Overcrowding occurs in some perennials as the root mass expands.) The best times to divide are after a plant has bloomed, or in the spring before much growth takes place, or in the fall as the plant foliage is dying back. If you divide for replanting, prune the top of the plant back. This will allow for new leaves to push from the crown and acclimate the plant to its new root size.

Hardening off and protecting your plants. When you buy a plant from a garden center it usually comes in a pot. Simply remove the pot and plant as described for trees and shrubs on page 87. If you've bought seedlings, or perhaps started them yourself, be sure to harden them off before transplanting them. Place the flats or pots outside during the day in a semi-protected area. Do this for a few days, up to a week, and your plants should be acclimated enough to be planted. In the North, if planting late in the fall, protecting newly planted perennials is a good idea. Simply using mulch hay or evergreen boughs will help to prevent crown heaving caused by alternate freezing and thawing. Remember not to mulch until after the first hard freeze.

Mulch. Mulch comes in many forms, such as shredded bark, pine needles, chopped leaves, grass clippings, and even newspaper. The primary benefit to plants in using mulch is moisture retention. A side benefit is the reduction in weeding. Shredded bark mulch has become very popular as an aesthetic element in the modern landscape. This is strictly a matter of taste in regard to its beauty, but it is definitely questionable what nitrogen value is being added through the use of bark. Don't use more than two inches around perennials. Amounts greater than this can cause damage or possible death to the plant, because of root suffocation. Usually the damage results from the forcing of the plant's roots closer to the surface. If this happens, they are far more susceptible to drought and frost damage.

Choice of Ground Covers

Ground covers are an important unifying element in the landscape. They provide solutions to some of the perplexing problems that the homeowner is likely to face in creating continuity in the yard. Grass is the most commonly used ground cover (and is discussed in more detail starting on page 99).

Ground covers come in a variety of heights and forms. Some shrubs and vines are also considered ground covers, such as junipers, cotoneaster, and euonymus. Often, however, ground covers are herbaceous and will die back to the ground in the late fall. In order to establish a dense growth of plants, you need to consider their spacing and growth rate when planting. Ground covers can also be effective in erosion control, and should be considered for any steep slope that is difficult to mow. They can substitute for grass in places where it doesn't grow, such as areas in full shade, or around trees and rocks — also preventing damage to, and from, the mower. Large amounts of low-growing ground plants can substitute for bark mulch and reduce the need for mulch replacement, not to mention a reduction in weeding.

Ground Covers: Value Added

Herbaceous plants, woody vines, and shrubs that cover the ground can contribute significant value to a home's landscape. It is important to remember that plants of this type are more costly per square foot to install and establish. You can ameliorate the cost by buying bareroot material, or by dividing and spreading existing plants that you have already planted. The payback is in reduced maintenance for bark mulch, bare soil, or lawn area.

Types of Alpine Plants

This is definitely a specialty type of garden, and is a relatively new hobby — probably only a couple of hundred years old. It demands the creation of a special soil environment that meets the needs of these very particular plants. Full sun, the placement of stones, and excellent drainage are essential for success with an alpine garden. For more information, we recommend that you consult a book on the subject.

Alpine Plants: Value Added

The value attributed to this type of garden is negligible and will probably appeal only to the enthusiast. If you were selling your home and a prospective owner was also an alpine plant enthusiast, an alpine garden could mean a quick sale (provided the garden looked good). The likelihood of this occuring is slim, to say the least. It is not a big market.

Open-Water and Bog Plants

These are plants that grow in wet places. Typical open-water plants are water lilies, and are usually found in ponds and garden pools. These

Ground covers are particularly useful as a unifying element in the landscape, connecting various areas of the yard.

can be quite beautiful to behold, but they are subject to their own peculiar maintenance needs. Bog plants are an even more specialized area of gardening, and include unusual plants such as insect eaters like sundews and pitcher plants. Sphagnum moss is another staple of the bog garden, as are numerous emergent plants.

Open-Water Plants: Value Added

This form of gardening is not likely to add significant value to your property because it's more suited to the enthusiast. If a water garden is well designed, properly installed, and conscientiously maintained, it can be very attractive for everyone. However, maintenance can be costly and time consuming. To the enthusiast, this is part of the appeal. Occasionally, they can become breeding grounds for mosquitoes and other biting flies. This is likely to be a problem only in an extensive water garden or pond.

There is a way in which this type of garden could be beneficial to you as a property owner. A wetland can stop the development of an entire commercial or residential project, so if there are wetlands next to your property, this can curb encroaching development. On the other hand, if you happen to have open land available that you would like to see converted into this type of an environment, you may be able to negotiate a pretty good deal: Sometimes a planning board or conservation commission will allow developers to "replace" the wetland areas they need to disturb with ones that they "create." If you are in the right place at the right time, you may be able to offer a win, win, and win proposition.

Woodland Plants and Wildflowers

Woodland plants and wildflowers are most commonly used in natural settings. It's important to have a relatively mature woods in place for woodland gardening. If you're interested in transforming an open area into a woodland garden, you need to be patient, because it will take years.

Tips for Planting Water Lilies

In areas where ice is a problem, or you are using a liner-style garden pool, plant the lilies in plastic buckets. This way you can remove them from the water in the fall. Prune the dead and dying foliage from the plants before storing and place them in a cool location where they will stay moist throughout the winter, but won't freeze. To help in retrieving the lilies in the fall, attach a fishing line and bobber to the bucket.

For northern water gardeners, preparing your pond for winter is done in October or November. During this time of heavy leaf fall, you can place a net or tarp over the water, then remove it when most of the leaves have dropped. This will save you from having to fish loads of leaves out of the pool area. You may want to leave your pump going until the water begins to freeze. It is very attractive to see the ice crystals form from a waterfall area, but be sure to pull it if the water freezes to where the pump is placed. The expanding ice could damage the internal works. (See chapter 7 for more information about installing water gardens.)

Certain wildflowers are found naturally in sunny areas and can be used in open spaces. There are many brands of wildflower seeds on the market, and you should check with your local nursery for those best suited to your area. Read the directions that accompany the seeds for the best results. It is also important to note the type of seeds in the mixture you purchase. You'll frequently find a blend of annuals, biennials, and perennials. This will determine to a large degree the sequence and the rate of bloom.

Woodland-plant and wildflower gardens generally improve as the years go by, provided that they're mowed once a year in the late fall.

In creating a wildflower garden, our experience has shown that it may be best to kill off all of the existing growth and to spray the area using a hydroseeding and mulching process. (Hydroseeding combines seed, water, and other agents to form a slurry that is sprayed on the soil surface; see the glossary for more information.) By covering the area before hydroseeding with a thick layer of newspapers, you can kill off existing growth without having to use pesticides. Call your local landscape contractor for further advice concerning this subject.

Woodland Plants: Value Added

The value provided by this group of plants is probably best recognized when these plantings are used as a substitute for lawns. This can apply to wooded areas where a lawn would have a more difficult time growing, as well as open, sunny fields where a meadow of wildflowers will require mowing only once or possibly twice in the course of a year.

Bulbs, Corms, and Tubers

Most people think of daffodils and tulips when they think of bulbs, but there is a broad selec-

Woodland plants and wildflowers are particularly useful on wooded property where it is difficult to maintain a lawn.

tion of spring-, summer-, and fall-flowering bulbs. Technically, many of our popular "bulbs" are properly named "corms" or "tubers." For our purposes, however, we refer to them all as bulbs. Some of the common spring bulbs (planted in the fall) are daffodil, crocus, tulip, scilla, hyacinth, grape hyacinth, anemone, winter aconite, leucojum, dwarf iris, and snowdrop. Summer-flowering bulbs include irises, caladiums, achimenes, cannas, lilies, fritillarias, begonias, gladioli, and dahlias. Fall bulbs are crocus, colchicum, and lycoris. This is not a complete list, but it does serve to show the many varieties available. The bulbs that will thrive best for you depend to a great degree upon your climate.

Bulbs: Value Added

The greatest value in spring-flowering bulbs may be the visual relief that you get after a long, cold winter! The color and texture of well-chosen and well-placed bulbs can be outstanding. If you are planning to sell your home at this time of year, they can be quite appealing to prospective buyers, and help sell the home. Remember, though, that this planting type requires forethought. You need to buy and plant the bulbs in the fall.

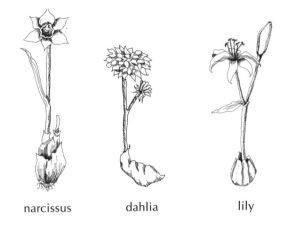

narcissus   dahlia   lily

Bulbs, corms, and tubers add color variety to your landscape, changing with the seasons.

Ferns, Mosses, Liverworts, and Lycopodiums

Non-flowering plants can be attractive additions to the shade garden. The display of green hues imparts a peaceful feeling. It's important to create the proper growing conditions. Generally speaking, all of these plants prefer an area of high humidity, with moist soils and shade in varying amounts. In most cases, the environment that you create will dictate the varieties that you're able to grow. Consult with your local nursery or garden center or any professional horticulturist.

Although ferns are generally available at nurseries and garden centers, it's next to impossible to find mosses, liverworts, and lycopodiums (or club moss) there. These plants can be collected from the wild if it's done responsibly. The best

Tips for Planting Bulbs

If you like the look of naturalized flowers — that is, flowers that look as if they were planted by nature, not by a gardener — a good method for the placement of bulbs is to go the area to be planted, grab a handful of bulbs, turn your back on the spot, and toss the bulbs over your head. Where they land is where you plant them.

The use of a bulb-planting tool will make the job much easier. Avoid using flimsy tools, since many bulb planters break or bend where the handle meets the planting tool portion.

If you are in an area with skunks around, don't use bonemeal when planting. Skunks are attracted to bonemeal and will dig the bulbs up to get at it. Fertilize with a 5–10–10 or similar formulation in the early and late spring.

If you have a problem with rodents, you can avoid losing bulbs by limiting your plantings to daffodils and other varieties of narcissus. Tulips and crocuses are delicacies to mice, voles, and chipmunks, but daffodils are poison.

By varying planting depths slightly, you can regulate the time of blooming by a few days. If you plant bulbs too deeply, however, they won't bloom. The proper depth varies according to the bulb. Deadheading or removing spent flowers from the bottom end of the flower stem will help to neaten the bulb bed and will contribute to the future vigor of the plants. Cut the stems back after they have started to turn brown and wither. Daffodils may also need to be divided every three to five years to maintain their vigor. This gives you the added benefit of increasing your plantings and gaining more color.

way is to collect spores from wild plants — this affects existing plants the least. You might take small plastic bags along with you on your next hike. Keep your eye open for mosses, liverworts, and lycopodiums in their spore-producing phase. Shake the spore capsules into the bag and take it back to your garden. Simply shake onto the prepared surfaces in shaded moist sites.

For some species of plants, you may have to wait a few years to see any results. In some cases, nothing will happen because certain plants can be very particular about aspects of their environment; for example, they may have a very limited pH range for optimum growth.

Another tip when collecting mosses is to dig them up in six-inch squares, leaving a checkerboard pattern. This will allow the remaining plants to grow back together, usually within just one season. Be sure that the collection site has a large area of undisturbed moss in addition to the specific place you're collecting from. Before doing any collecting, also be sure to let the landowner know of your intentions and be sure to get his or her permission. One good place to collect can be wooded areas that are slated for construction and are going to be razed.

MAKING A "WET WALL"

An interesting project that may add significant value to your property is the construction of what is called a "wet wall." It can be done in the confines of a greenhouse or in a region that is not subject to too many deep freezes. Ultimately what you will create is a valley of ferns and mosses with nooks and crannies and sitting areas. This is done by first creating a space between two walls made of masonry blocks. The distance between the walls should be greater the higher you go. The height of the walls should be taller by about a foot than the tallest person visiting the space.

Vary the spacing at ground level and create an alcove or two. Use large, flat stones as a walking and activity surface. A pool and waterfall might be attractive as well. Create ledges and shelves in the ascending wall. Leave some of them open and fill with soil, and place into others some sizable pieces of flat, natural stone. Try to mimic the natural geology of your region. Coat some of the stones with sulfur in order to modify the pH and then install a drip irrigation system on top of the wall and let the water seep down onto and into the blocks.

Put a shade cloth temporarily over the entire space and plant trees on the outside edges. These trees will eventually produce sufficient shade to replace the shade cloth. Sprinkle spores and plant wild mosses, ferns, and other non-flowering plants on the blocks and stones in this private space. On the hottest days you will soon have a private, sound-buffered, and cool and shady retreat for an escape.

Non-Flowering Plants: Value Added

This addition to your landscape can be extremely valuable because it provides luxuriant growth where other plants may fail.

Vegetable/Herb Gardens

Vegetable and herb gardens have always enjoyed immense popularity in American culture. One reason is the personal gratification of growing your own produce. Herbs offer beauty, food seasoning, and medicinal properties. The major problems with these types of gardens is the high maintenance required. However, you can significantly reduce the amount of maintenance by good planning and the use of raised beds. (See "For Further Reading" at the back of this book for resources.)

Herbs and certain vegetables can also be incorporated into your annual and perennial gardens. Many people with smaller yards find that growing vegetables, herbs, and flowers in containers is very gratifying. Obviously, this requires little space, but provides you with the opportunity to enhance decks, patios, walkways, swimming pools, entryways, and other difficult-to-landscape areas.

Vegetable/Herb Gardens: Value Added

The value derived from these types of gardens is limited to a relatively small group of people. These are people who like to "get their hands dirty." They feel a great deal of satisfaction from growing their own produce and their own herbs for cooking and home remedies — not to mention natural dyes and fibers for weaving. For a number of people, however, the thought of having to maintain a food garden is a horrifying proposition. They would far rather go to the supermarket to harvest their veggies and the drugstore to get their medicines. As a buyer or a seller of a home, though, don't let this deter you from having one. It is very easy to convert a lawn to a vegetable or herb garden, and vice versa.

Lawns

A beautiful carpet of green lawn can do a great deal for the entire landscape. It provides contrast to the plantings of shrubs and trees, and creates a great place for the family to play. By providing open space, it helps to define the entire yard and garden. It is truly one of the best unifying elements in your landscape. When we do a complete landscape, it is the last component of the installation because there is less disturbance to the site.

The biggest problem with lawns is that they require so much maintenance. The reason that they're used so extensively is because of easy installation and low initial cost. Therefore, we

A lush, green lawn out front adds a great deal to a house's curb appeal.

recommend considering other ground covers in areas where they may be more appropriate. It's possible to do this over time. You can install a lawn and then kill off portions of it to plant the alternative ground cover. In the long run, this will reduce your maintenance and allow more time to enjoy your spectacular yard.

A variety of lawn grasses is used throughout the country, because of the broad range of growing conditions. A variety of transitional grasses can be used in both warm and cool climates. This is true of all plants.

It's important to note that the insects and diseases that you may encounter will vary from region to region as well. Establish a good relationship with your local nursery or garden center, where you can find help with your trials and tribulations.

Lawn: Value Added

There is nothing like a lush, green lawn to provide the curb appeal that will attract the potential home buyer. People with families find it important to have open areas for activities such as volleyball and badminton. As a design element, a beautiful lawn becomes the unifying element of a single texture that helps to frame the home and other structures.

This value is, of course, offset by the regular maintenance that a lawn requires. Chapter 9 offers some guidance on ways you may be able to cut down on the drudgery.

Tips and Techniques for Softscape Construction

For many of us, our enthusiasm for landscape does not match our pocketbooks. Although there is nothing like employing a landscape pro for doing those tough jobs around the yard, some of us get our recreation from doing the work ourselves or can't afford to have the in-stallation done by others. The biggest drawback to this approach is that the time it takes for one person to do the work can drag out for years. To some, that is an attractive prospect — they always like to have a project going. To others it could be a nightmare. If, however, you fall into the former category, you will enjoy the following tips:

Compost

In developing the planting beds in your landscape, you need to make a rich medium in which the roots of your plantings will thrive. An inexpensive way to do this is to incorporate your own compost into the ground. Compost can be made from your own garbage as well as leaves, grass clippings, and ground-up vegetable garden debris. Composting takes time and knowledge — your local university or Extension Service will have information on composting, or check a reference book. The use of earthworms, or vermiculture, has become popular as a way to accelerate the composting process.

Sources for Perennials

If you want to start a perennial garden, talk to neighbors and friends with perennial gardens and offer your help in dividing their plants in exchange for some of the divided plants.

Using Cuttings

Buy a package of the three strengths of rooting hormone. Hormex is one brand name. With this investment, you can start your own plants from cuttings. This does not work effectively for all plants; however, it works on enough of them to make it worth your while. An important thing to remember is to take the cuttings from vertical-growth twigs. If you use lateral-growth twigs, you will end up with plants that do not grow true to form.

Using Seed

Start some of your plants from collected seed. However, remember that when you grow plants from seed you can't be sure of what you will get from the seed. It is essential that you read about seed germination requirements. Some seeds, for example, need to be frozen for a certain period of time in order to grow (it's called "stratification"). You can simulate this process by placing the seeds in the freezer for the appropriate amount of time.

Transplanting

Learn how and when to transplant. The time to root-prune (explained below) and the time to move plants is determined by the type of plants you are moving. Your success depends on learning and using the correct techniques, but when you do, a whole world of native-plant gathering will be opened to you. As we have mentioned elsewhere, *get permission first!* It is also important to note that you should *not* take any plants on the endangered species list — find out what they are.

Root-Pruning Transplants

Root-prune wild shrubs and trees about a year in advance of transplanting for greater success. The root systems of wild plants can range over great distances. By pruning the roots all around the plant, and to a size you feel comfortable moving, you will start the production of new roots closer to the base of the plant. This will allow you to dig the plant more easily and will help prevent the rootball from falling apart.

Sources

Good sources of transplant stock, cutting stock, or seed are the local Cooperative Exten-sion Service, friends, relatives, or neighbors. You could also check with your town or city for landowners with large tracts of land, or get their names from the town tax maps.

Planting Programs

Some towns have special, subsidized tree-planting programs. Call your city arborist or tree warden for more detail. You might also talk to some of the civic organizations in your community, such as the Boy and Girl Scouts, Lions Club, or garden clubs, about their programs for beautifying your area.

Wood Chip Mulch

A possible source of free wood chip mulch is your local professional tree company. To find a company that produces a large volume of this type of material, call your electric utility and ask who does the trim work under power lines.

Manure

Talk to local equestrian groups or farmers for access to their manure. Most of the time, it is yours for the cost of hauling it away. Do not use green manure — compost it for at least one year.

Staking

Cut up old rubber hoses to cover the wires you use for guying trees, where the wire would touch the tree. Flag the wires with surveyor's tape or bright ribbon to keep people from tripping over them.

Using a Tarp

Before digging a planting hole, put a plastic tarp or ground cloth on the ground. Place all of the excavated earth on the tarp. This makes for easy cleanup, less loss of valuable soil, and a reduction in the spreading of fresh weed seeds.

Tools

Borrow or buy a long-handled shovel — most people find it easier to dig holes with one of these than with a short- or D-handled shovel. It gives you better leverage and makes tossing the material you have dug easier. When preparing trees or shrubs for transplanting, be sure to use a transplanting or root-pruning spade. This differs from a normal shovel because it has an extra-long, narrow, and flat blade. Make sure that the blade is very sharp when using.

Using an Antidesiccant

Spray an antidesiccant on broad-leaved evergreens before transplanting to prevent moisture loss from the plant. An antidesiccant seals in valuable moisture by coating the leaf with a waxlike substance. Be sure to read the directions carefully — it is not a material to be sprayed on all plants, and it is relatively expensive. Remember that the leaves' stomata, or breathing tubes, are on the undersurface and not the top.

Know Your Root Structure

The rootball of some plants, such as rhododendrons, azaleas, and Japanese maples, is shallow and wide, not deep. Research the plants that you are digging so you'll know their root structures.

When to Transplant

Research has shown us that some plants transplant well only during certain times of the year. Find out from your local nursery before you transplant.

Make Notes

Keep a notebook handy and write down any ideas you have or tips from professionals. Before long you will have a handy reference tool for helping you improve your plantings.

Tips and Techniques for Planting Trees and Shrubs

Remember that your plant's rootball will probably either be wrapped in burlap with a wire cage (for larger plants), simply wrapped in burlap with twine binding it together, in a plastic pot, or bareroot. Planting techniques will vary with the size of the plant and the type of root wrap. The following planting principles remain the same, however, whether it's a twenty- foot-tall tree or a one-gallon potted flower.

Digging the hole. When planting, be sure that your holes are wide but not too deep. The depth of the hole should be shallower than the depth of the rootball by about one inch, so that when you plant the tree or large shrub, the top of the rootball will be an inch higher than the surrounding grade. This allows for the settling that will occur, particularly with larger plants.

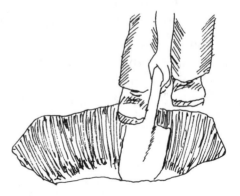

Dig a hole that is 1 inch shallower than the depth of the tree's rootball.

Placing the plant in the hole. When your hole is dug and the plant is next to it, carefully place the plant into the hole. When you're lowering the tree into the hole, be careful not to drop it. Sometimes it's best to slide the tree into place, holding onto the burlap wrapping. For large tree with the rootball wrapped in a wire cage, we recommend that you do the following. First, lower the tree into the hole using the wire cage. Then remove the top two-thirds of the wire, using bolt cutters. Next take off the burlap in that area. Again, use caution — it is of the utmost importance that the rootball remain intact. Last of all, cut slits where possible in the remaining burlap. Everything else is the same for large or smaller trees. You should have your hose handy with a soft spray nozzle for watering the tree after the hole is filled in.

Note: Prune off any damaged roots or roots that look like they will wrap around the tree as they grow (girdling roots).

Do not twist the tree in the hole, because this can cause the roots to grow in a circle around the tree. This can girdle the tree or cause the tree to be susceptible to wind damage, because the roots don't develop correctly; it is particularly true in heavy soils.

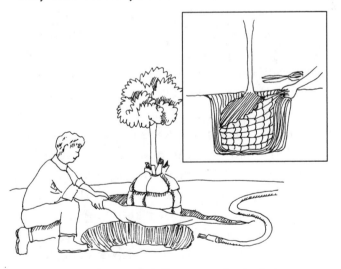

One way to lower the plant into the hole is to slide it into place on a piece of burlap wrapping. Once in place, cut slits in the remaining burlap (see detail).

Amending the soil. Two major schools of thought have developed for amending the soil used in planting. The first approach is to use additives such as peat moss, manure, and lime (when appropriate) for an individual hole. However, some people don't do this amending, because they feel that if the plant gets everything it needs in the small area of the dug hole it will not send roots out into the surrounding soils, and it will become susceptible to blowover. If you do follow the amending method, we recommend that you look carefully at the soil structure where you are planting and try to match similar textures and organic content with that soil. Be sure you know the soil's pH before applying lime or sulfur.

Both methods are used, so we suggest you do the following. When you're planting a tree, do not use any additives. Use only the native loam or soil from the hole if possible. Invariably, when you dig a hole and plant a tree, you'll need some extra loam. Purchase some loam if necessary, but use it in the very top part of the hole. If you must buy loam for planting, don't add anything to the soil, with the exception of additives for raising or lowering the pH. Use lime for raising the pH, and sulfur for lowering. (See chapter 12 and the glossary for more information about pH.)

We should point out that when you're creating a whole bed, or an entire planting medium that stands on its own, it is advisable to amend the soil. So when you're planting in ground that has been stripped of loam, or you're double-digging for a perennial bed, we advocate the amending process.

If you need to amend the soil, use additives that match the texture and organic content of the surrounding soil.

Filling the hole. You're now ready to place the soil around the tree's rootball. Fill the hole about a fourth of the way up its side, then water the area thoroughly. After watering, firmly tamp the loam. Be sure not to jump up and down in this tamping process, but step down firmly. The water helps to rid the hole of air pockets which can be very detrimental or fatal to the tree because they can dry out roots and root hairs.

After tamping, fill the hole two-thirds full with loam, then water, creating a "moat," and then tamp as before, after the water has drained. Fill the rest of the hole and do a final tamping. At this point we like to create a dish to hold water around the base of the tree. At the outside rim of the hole, form a two-inch-high dam out of soil with your hands. We then like to use shredded and screened softwood mulch around the base of the tree. It should be no deeper than three to four inches around the plant (do not pile mulch against the stem) and about six inches in depth around the outside of the planting hole.

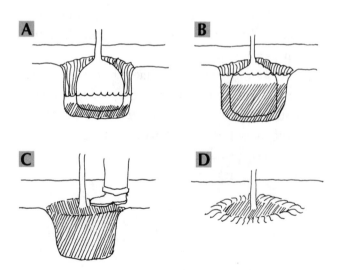

Filling the hole around the rootball involves a gradual process of adding loam (A), watering (B), and tamping it down (C). Finally, you create a dish around the trunk (D) to hold water.

Protection. It's an excellent idea to maintain a weed-free ring of at least three feet around a young tree or shrub. Use a good-quality mulch to help reduce the need for extensive watering. Another strong recommendation is to cover the bottom of the trunk of smooth-barked plants, particularly fruit trees, with a sleeve or screen of wire or paper called a "mouse guard." The mouse guard protects the plant during the winter, when mice burrow in the snow to get at the bark of trees — especially apple trees, lilacs, burning bushes, and crab apples — when other food supplies are short. Adjust or remove as the tree matures.

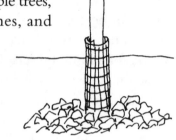

A mouse guard helps protect the trunk of a young tree during the winter.

Staking. If you have planted a large tree you may want to stake it. The primary reason for staking is to keep the tree from blowing over in high winds. The best candidates for staking are evergreens and large deciduous trees, since they catch the wind in their branches and leaves. If the tree is planted in the early summer, it's generally not necessary to stake, but for planting in the late summer or fall, we highly recommend it. One growing season is more than sufficient to leave the stakes or guys on. It is to the detriment of the tree to leave them on any longer — the guy wires might girdle the tree, or the tree can become reliant on the staking to support it instead of producing sufficient anchoring roots. Never place bare wire against the bark of any tree or shrub; always encase the wire in rubber hose where it touches the bark. Be sure to use real rubber hose and not vinyl hose — vinyl is a brittle material and can be abrasive.

The type of staking depends on the size of the tree. Extremely large trees may require additional anchoring such as with deadmen or duck-bill anchors — something best left to the professionals. (See the glossary for more information.)

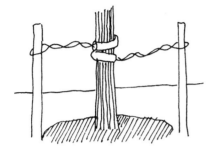

Staking helps prevent a tree from being blown over by high winds.

Watering a new tree. Water is the "poor man's fertilizer," and is the lifeblood of the tree or shrub. Be sure that it receives adequate amounts, but be careful not to overwater.

We recommend a method called "deep watering" — turning on the hose so that the water trickles out of the end. The idea is to water the plant deeply and slowly, because the ground absorbs water at a slow rate. The rate is determined by the looseness of the soil — sandy soil will absorb water more quickly, but won't hold it as long as a heavier clay-based soil. Generally, a tree should be watered one to two times a week for fifteen to twenty minutes per watering. A shrub should receive water for five to ten

It is best to water a tree deeply and slowly.

minutes twice a week initially. Remember that the rootball is anywhere from one foot down to three feet deep, so watering just the surface will not do the job.

Repeat this procedure for at least two weeks. After three weeks, water as needed. The plant should not be allowed to dry out for an extended period of time. If it doesn't rain for five to six days, you should be thinking about watering on the seventh. If you will have difficulty in getting water to the plant, you should consider the application of an anti-desiccant (as described on page 102). Another option is to strip the leaves from the plant at the time of planting, which prevents it from losing moisture. New leaves will appear in time.

Signs that might indicate moisture fatigue are wilting leaves, yellowing leaf margins, browning tips, premature leaf or needle drop, and overall poor color.

A commonly held misconception is that when a plant goes dormant — that is, drops its leaves or needles — in the fall, it no longer needs to be watered. Nothing could be farther from the truth. In lieu of sufficient rain, you must continue watering until the ground freezes. A plant going into the winter with a dry rootball, especially a newly planted one, may die. The reason you may not need to water as much in the fall is that water evaporates less in cooler temperatures. Also, in the fall in many parts of the country, more moisture is available naturally. If you have a dry fall, beware of underwatering.

Pruning a new tree. Pruning at the time of planting is very controversial, with many differences of opinion. Our experience has brought us to the following recommendations:

- When you plant, prune only dead or broken branches.
- Be sure not to prune the central leader on a tree!

After a tree becomes established, you can see whether there is sufficient support from the root system for the amount of canopy; portions of the tree will die if there isn't. At this time you can prune and feel confident that you're taking out the appropriate branches. This is also the time to remove any crossing branches or too-close stems.

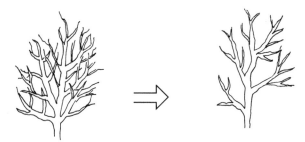

Prune branches to the collar of the branch, so you don't have stumps protruding from the trunk.

Some general rules of pruning:

- When pruning, keep in mind the ultimate shape you are trying to accomplish.
- Always prune to the collar of the branch. This is the area that connects the branch to the trunk or a smaller branch to the larger one. It will usually have a slight swelling and a different bark pattern from the stem or trunk.
- Don't leave stumps. After you have pruned, you should be looking at a small stub — the collar. You should not leave a couple of inches of wood protruding from the trunk.
- Don't leave ragged cuts with bark hanging down or ripped off the plant. Be sure to undercut when pruning any large branch. You can also hold onto the branch to minimize bark tearing, unless that branch is too large for you to close your fingers around.
- Always prune from a stable surface and always have a clear path of escape.

- Anything you can't reach from the ground comfortably should be left to the professionals.

Weed-control fabric. For shrubs in bed areas, consider the use of a weed-control fabric. We recommend this material in beds where the plants will grow together, forming an overall mass, such as low-growing junipers used as a ground cover. Don't use black plastic. It doesn't allow for gas exchange or permeation of water, and in times of drought will cause a plant's roots to grow near the surface, which will make them susceptible to winterkill.

Mulch. Mulch comes in many forms, such as shredded bark, pine needles, chopped leaves, grass clippings, and even newspaper. The primary benefit of mulch is moisture retention. A side benefit is the reduction in weeding. Shredded bark mulch has become very popular as an aesthetic element in the modern landscape. This is strictly a matter of taste as far as its beauty is concerned. Don't use any more than two inches around perennials and four inches around shrubs and trees. Any more can cause damage or possible death to the plant, because of root suffocation. Another important point is not to pile mulch up against the stem or crown of a woody plant. This can hold moisture against the bark and cause the bark to split and crack, which may make the plant more prone to insect infestation and winterkill.

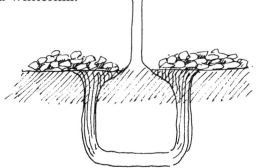

When you apply mulch around the base of a tree or shrub, do not pile it up against the stem or trunk.

9

Investing in Sustainable Landscape Alternatives

IN RECENT YEARS, AN ENVIRONMENTAL MOVE-ment has been making itself known in a variety of industries. The movement is known as "sustainable development," and it is starting to gain recognition in the landscape industry. It finds its roots in design disciplines such as permaculture — the concept that the farther the landscape is from the house, the lower the maintenance it should require — as well as the recycling movement, and its popularity is gaining momentum, as indicated by the following:

- In 1995, President Clinton alluded to it in his advocacy for including "native" plants in federally funded landscape projects.
- The Environmental Protection Agency has developed a set of environmentally

and economically sound practices for the landscape industry to be used in conjunction with federally funded projects.
- Sustainability was the focus of a Maine-watch Institute report in 1990, and a University of Southern Maine publication and conference in 1993, as well as state legislation in that year.
- In 1994, in Maine, statewide hearings on sustainability were sponsored by the Department of Economic and Community Development.
- The overall theme of the 1995 State of the World Report produced by the World-watch Institute was sustainability.
- Active organizations such as Sustainable Maine and Sustainable Florida are also making their voices heard.

What Is a Sustainable Approach to Landscaping?

Sustainable development was defined by the World Commission on the Environment and Development in 1986 as "development which meets the needs of the present without compromising the ability of future generations to meet their own needs." According to Kent Redford, Director of Conservation, Science & Stewardship/Latin American & Caribbean Division of The Nature Conservancy, everything we do on the planet affects the ecology in some way. If we can understand what these costs are, we can better create compromises that are for the greater good of not only the earth but also the physical needs of humanity.

Why is this so important to the value of a home? Reducing the amount of waste generated and using fewer goods and services will save money at all levels. It is true that maintenance can have its therapeutic aspects, and there may actually be a case for spending some amount of time mowing and weeding and trimming and pruning and so forth. However, by having a sustainable landscape, and by using sustainable practices in building and maintaining that landscape, you contribute to the general well-being of the environment while simultaneously keeping money in your pocket to spend in some other way.

A sustainable approach to landscaping specifies direction and execution that reduce the expenditure of energy in the near and long-term future. This approach also means that the executed design will be self-maintaining or will require very little maintenance. Some of the landscape paradigms common today are far from sustainable and require massive amounts of time and energy in order to maintain any aesthetic appeal.

The Pros and Cons of Sustainable Landscapes

Property owners don't request sustainable landscapes for two basic reasons. The first reason is that the construction of high-maintenance landscapes is relatively inexpensive and the second is an ignorance of sustainable alternatives and their economic benefits. In many cases, that ignorance extends to landscape designers as well. We find old ways to be comfortable and change to be hard. Besides, a low-maintenance landscape may not be in the best interest of the design company if, as a contractor, it offers maintenance services. If the designer works for a planting contractor, reducing or eliminating amendments and other materials might mean the loss of profits received on material goods that are sold as a part of the job. However, most designers have been consciously moving in the direction of sustainability, by virtue of their desire to do what is best for the plant communities they create.

WHAT DOES "SUSTAINABLE" MEAN?

The definition of *sustainable* varies widely according to the discipline to which it is being applied. For landscaping, it can be defined as follows: *A state, criterion, or condition that reduces the energy or physical labor necessary for maintaining a pleasing aesthetic appearance while fulfilling its functional role.*

Ideally, the goal is a self-sustaining environment where plants are living in harmony with each other and are not subject to stress and the resulting diseases and harmful insects.

Designing and Building a Sustainable Landscape

A sustainable landscape design seeks alternatives to commonly held beliefs and approaches. For example, two popular elements of modern American landscapes are the lawn and the mulched plant bed. On the basis of square-footage costs for installation, both of them are relatively inexpensive, especially if the lawn is seeded. Once installed, however, they demand a certain level of maintenance. A lawn has to be kept uniform in color, texture, and height. Mulched planting beds have to be kept weed-free, consistent in texture, and attractive in color. When you examine the expected life of either of these elements and you apply the sum total of the associated maintenance costs, you find that the cost per square foot rises dramatically. If you were to apply the hidden environmental costs of applied maintenance, the cost would go out of sight.

Elements Required for Traditional Built Landscape

Grass lawns and mulched beds are not the only high-maintenance features of the traditional built landscape. Following is a list of all the typical elements and the tasks or supplies they require to maintain beauty and function:

- **Lawn.** Fertilizer, pesticides, mowing, liming, raking, trimming, edging, de-thatching, core aeration, repair, replacement
- **Shrubs.** Pruning, shearing, fertilizer, wrapping, pest control, mulching
- **Trees.** Staking, pruning, cabling, bracing, fertilizer, wrapping, pest control, mulching
- **Planting beds.** Weeding, mulching, edging
- **Annuals.** Weeding, deadheading, fertilizer, mulch, replanting
- **Perennials.** Weeding, deadheading, thinning, dividing, staking, fertilizer, mulching, pest control
- **Bulbs.** Replacement, fertilizer, storage, dividing
- **Hardscape.** Repairs, snow removal, replacements, painting, etc.

It is fairly evident that a landscape can be a significant drain on energy resources, such as gasoline and oil, not to mention time and labor. We will look at the three landscape areas — design, construction, and maintenance — for ways to reduce these requirements.

The Aesthetics of a Sustainable Design

If you want to use a sustainable approach to designing your landscape, you need to consider certain aesthetics. Even though sustainability focuses on environmental considerations, it also takes into account how the landscape can enhance the quality of life for yourself — and for the people who may eventually purchase your home — in more than environmental terms. These benefits include the scale of the landscape at maturity (for example, the feeling that a large shade tree provides is more powerful than that of the same tree as a sapling), enclosures or areas for escape, vistas or other created views in the landscape, a sense of destination, a way of involving all the senses (not only sight) and the emotions, and the physical needs of the people who use the landscape.

Designing for Environmental Benefits

Environmental considerations are at the core of sustainable landscaping. A sustainable approach challenges "standard operating procedures" in creating a design that responds to site conditions. To deal with the land responsibly and knowledgeably, you have to consider a large number of variables. It is simpler to have a quick solution that might ignore reality, but the efficacy of the fix will prove to leave a great deal to be desired.

One outstanding example is soil, often referred to as "dirt" or "loam." Soil is a dynamic element that can have a dramatic impact on the success of a lawn or other plantings, when used properly. We have seen over the years any number of types of soil passed off as "loam." You need to consider many aspects of soil in order to be sure you have the "right stuff" in place. The first among these is texture — determined by the proportions of sand, silt, and clay in the soil's makeup. A second important element is the percentage of organic matter in the soil. A third is the carbon/nitrogen ratio, and a fourth essential consideration is pH (the soil's acidity or alkalinity). The proper balance of these four in a soil means considerably less input of fertilizers and "corrective services" in order to grow a healthy, viable lawn and vigorous landscape plants.

Other important environmental factors that affect sustainability are drainage and site exposure. When consulting on a design for a property, we usually ask if there are any drainage problems. Invariably, the answer is yes. The impact of the landscape on drainage as well as the impact of drainage on the landscape is not often considered in the design planning. A better understanding of civil engineering by more designers would go a long way toward solving this problem. A great deal of time and money can be wasted in addressing drainage concerns after the fact. It takes very little time or money to correct the problem in the very beginning.

Understanding the site's exposure and installing the landscape accordingly will also save you considerable money. Wind, snow cover, slope, hardiness zone, and the amount of available light all influence exposure. If these factors are not considered, you may be subjecting your plantings to considerable stress, if not death. As stated before, this stress will lead to attacks by insects and diseases, which in turn lead to costly treatments (see chapter 8 for more information).

Horticultural Considerations

A wide range of horticultural choices also needs to be considered in creating sustainable landscaping that reduces environmental and monetary costs. For instance, if you pay attention to plant growth form, you can reduce the amount of shearing or pruning required, by choosing the plant that grows naturally in the shape you want for that space. If you are aware of growth rate, you can avoid the use of a plant that quickly outgrows its space and needs constant trimming or, finally, replacing. Some shrubs work well in a mass planting — you can reduce the side trimming and enhance the mass effect at the same time. For planting in a specific area in the landscape, you need to choose plants that are compatible with each other and avoid juxtaposing plants with entirely different cultural needs. Also, some trees have a tendency toward weak crotches, thin and easily sunscalded bark, or even girdling roots. By avoiding the use of these plants you can eliminate costly remedies in the future, not to mention emotional stress to yourself. Certain types of fruit production from plants can create seasonal messes that will require expenditure of time, money, and labor to clean up. Other types of plants can be large producers of unwanted "offspring" that more categorically can be called weeds. (Additional discussion of these factors can be found in chapter 8.)

Sustainable Construction Techniques

Building a sustainable landscape means paying attention to the source of your materials, so that you are aware not only of cost but also that your purchases are environmentally friendly in the way they have been produced and in the way they will be used. Ideally, a good source is local, reliable, and "green" (ecologically sound) in conducting business. For instance, instead of buying expensive bark mulch, you may consider using the chippings that come from line trimming crews working for the local utility company. These will provide more nitrogen to your plants, and many times you can get the material for free. It isn't as pretty as a bagged mulch or processed bark mulch, but within a few months, no mulch looks particularly good. (See pages 92–93 in chapter 8 for additional suggestions on how to save money and be kind to the environment and the general health of your landscape at the same time.)

It does not always follow that recycled or "green" products cost less, in which case the choice is less obvious and is driven by your own priorities. Regardless, it's a good idea to look at all the options for materials, designs, or procedures, and not to choose automatically what "always has been done."

One good example is in the planting of shrubs and trees. Almost every gardening or landscape book will tell you that you should put amendments in with a new planting, such as peat moss, fertilizer, cow manure, or other similar material. This implies that every planting hole or plant is exactly the same. This is far from true. In many circumstances, no amendments at all may be preferred. Generally speaking, the fewer transition zones that a plant's roots have to go through, the better.

Maintaining a Sustainable Landscape

Many times a landscape is designed with little thought to the maintenance it will require. The design process focuses on aesthetics and function, but overlooks efficiency or ease of maintenance. Often, this is because designers don't have practical experience in hands-on yard or garden maintenance. For example, a designer might want to create an undulating plant bed surrounded by lawn, but doesn't consider how difficult mowing will be; or a designer likes the sculptural form of a particular tree, but doesn't think about the messy fruit that it pelts pedestrians with.

Insect and Disease Problems

Some of the biggest problems in landscape plantings are caused by insects and disease. Good design can reduce both of these by placing plants where they will have the most favorable growing conditions. Unhealthy or "stressed" plants tend to be more susceptible to insects and disease. A good sustainable solution uses a "bio-organic" approach. Two programs with this approach that are now popular in the United States are known as Integrated Pest Management and Plant Health Care. IPM is probably the better known of the two. A far more sensible approach than the usual treatment with chemicals and pesticides, IPM looks at effective alternative biological solutions and monitors for the presence of pests before responding with chemical spray — for example, using ladybugs to control aphids or dragonflies to control mosquitoes. PHC has a tendency to be less reactive than IPM, and seeks to improve growing conditions that may lead to the existence of pest problems in the first place. For example, if the soil is compacted, PHC may recommend the use of a "grow gun" to fracture the soil and allow better gas exchange. If soil compaction is widespread, PHC may recommend the use of alternative plants or even architectural solutions instead of plants. In IPM, the pests are managed; in PHC, the plant's health is managed.

Hands-Off Maintenance

A final approach involves no cost at all, although the results are questionable. We call this "total hands-off" — no mowing, trimming, weeding, etc. Hands-off maintenance will mean an evolution for the plants in your landscape, with many invasions and die-offs. This approach is definitely not for everyone or every circumstance, as it may produce a property that is an eyesore. Most towns and cities have ordinances mandating a minimum of maintenance on any publicly viewed area. Fines can be assessed if you don't heed these laws — as one of the authors, Richard Dubé, can attest.

◾ ◾ ◾

"I once lived a couple of doors down from the mayor of the town. I grass-whipped an area ten feet around the house for access, and let the rest grow naturally. I was studying and photographing the evolution of the lawn and the new plants that emerged. I even had some prairie wildflowers. The mayor did not take kindly to my 'experiment' and passed a statute that said all lawns had to be kept mowed at a certain minimum height. I was served notice by the constable and had to put an end to my studies."

◾ ◾ ◾

More Maintenance Considerations

Early maintenance of trees prevents future problems and expense. If you prune out deadwood and crossing branches within a year of planting you will reduce many problems that will be more costly down the road. It is also a good time to remove branches that form a weak crotch, which can fail when the tree is bigger — branches can break and fall off. A couple of clips with a hand snippers when the tree is still small will prevent a costly remedy later.

The need for an irrigation system indicates that the landscape is not sustaining itself. If the plantings are in balance with the site's characteristics, there should be no need to supplement watering. If your trees, shrubs, and perennials

Sustainable landscape lawn alternatives include replacing grass with ground covers. This requires a lot of work the first year, but is much easier to maintain than a lawn in the long run.

are dying from desiccation because the natural rainfall in your area is insufficient, then it is likely you have the wrong types of plants. Here you should replace moisture-loving plants with drought-tolerant plants.

Overhead irrigation systems are the most common type, and operate on computerized or windup timers. Although more costly to install, saturation systems with "smart pumps" are the most efficient. Monitors in the soil indicate when the system needs to provide moisture. Water stored in an underground cistern is pumped directly into the soil through pipes or tiles. Batteries that run the pumps are solar powered and regenerated with sunlight. This system is quiet, and once it is set up it costs nothing to run and little to maintain. (More information about irrigation systems is in chapters 7 and 12.)

Rethinking the Traditional American Landscape

As we have already said, a sustainable landscape approach seeks alternatives to commonly held beliefs and approaches. Here are some alternatives to lawns, mulched plant beds, and other traditional elements of the American landscape.

Alternatives to Lawns

Lawns have no place in a truly self-sustaining landscape since they require so much care. Yet, it is not likely that the American public is about to give up anytime soon on its love affair with the grass lawn. As a nation, we invest millions of dollars as well as time and energy in keeping lawns a pristine green. Besides, there are good practical reasons for a lawn in the landscape. They are good surfaces for badminton, croquet, volleyball, and golf, as well as for many other activities. From a design perspective, lawns offer an attractive static element in the landscape that can provide framing, contrast of color and texture, or transition for the eye.

From a sustainable perspective, however, lawns are anathema. Think of the amounts of fertilizer, pesticide, and water demanded by grass (especially most of the popular cultivars of bluegrass). Consider all of the gasoline that is burned up by lawn mowers and weed-eaters, and the resulting emissions. What measures does a sustainable approach use to lessen or eliminate time and money spent on a lawn? Here are a few suggestions:

- Reduce the area used by lawns. Too often, lawns are there just to fill space.
- Replace lawn with alternative ground covers where there is no need for activity or sports.
- Use alternative grass-seed mixtures that reduce or eliminate the need for constant mowing, fertilizing, pesticides, and watering.
- Manage the lawn as an ecosystem and apply cultural practices that will enhance rather than inhibit the lawn ecosystem.

Alternatives to Bark Mulch

The other high-maintenance aspect of typical (surburban and urban) landscapes is the mulched plant bed. Twelve to fourteen years ago, bark mulch was given away as a waste product. When it was first offered for sale, the price was around $2 per cubic yard. Now, the price is almost double the price of loam.

What is so appealing about bark mulch? As with most things aesthetic, it is really quite subjective. Some people like red mulch, some like their mulch almost black, and some like their mulch chunky. But any way you serve it, most people like mulch. It is even given an aura of respectability by landscape contractors who rightfully point out the benefits and advantages of a mulched bed — it helps to retain moisture for the plants, it can inhibit weeds from germinating in exposed soil, and in time it will add organic matter to the soil as it breaks down. However, from a sustainability perspective, mulch creates problems:

- It provides a medium for encouraging weed development and growth.
- If the mulch layer increases, it can encourage roots to come closer to the surface and make the plants more susceptible to drought.
- There is the continuous cost of "topping off the mulch" to maintain an attractive color, as well as the eventual cost of extricating an overabundance of the mulch.
- Bark mulch does little to no good in reintroducing nitrogen into the soil.

In the sustainable landscape, mulch is used only with the first planting to take advantage of the benefits it does offer. To fill voids and provide an overall even texture, ground covers can be used instead of mulch. Ideally, these ground covers are assertive, but not aggressive, and would not compete with shrub and tree root systems — as some lawns do. (See chapter 8 for more information about ground cover choices.) Shrubs planted together in beds and allowed to grow en masse will also eliminate the need for pruning, weeding, and mulch replenishment.

Other Alternatives to Traditional Landscaping

Long-term plant relationships and cultural compatibility is another area within our traditional approach to landscaping that can be challenged. A good example in the Northeast is the relationship between white pine and lawns. The pine creates an acid condition that runs counter to the needs of the lawn, which will stop growing, thin out, and allow acid-loving weeds to proliferate. The homeowner limes the lawn in response and changes the soil pH to more alkaline. This is the opposite of what the pine needs and may put it under stress, resulting in insect problems. A continuing cycle of response and care is created that could have been averted by planting a buffering ground cover under and around the tree. Another option is a tree more compatible with the needs of the lawn.

Many other traditional landscape elements can be challenged. For example, soil is a dynamic and complex system. Some important factors, often overlooked, include the carbon-to-nitrogen ratio in the soil, the porosity of the soil, the earthworms per cubic foot, or even the percentage of organic matter. Understanding these factors will help you create a healthy soil environment, which leads to healthy plants.

Gradually Transforming an Existing Landscape

Even if your property has already been landscaped, it can be converted to a more sustainable approach. Before you do this, though, you need to know what it is you have to work with. The following process will help to guide you through the process of determining what your options are and to show you where you are wasting money, time, and labor.

1. Do an environmental audit of the grounds. (See the Environmental Audit on pages 115–116).
2. List your goals and possible corrections as determined by the audit.
3. Prioritize your goals and corrections.
4. Determine a cost/benefit analysis with a payback cycle on your proposed corrections.
5. Establish an action plan with a timeline that runs from initiation through completion.
6. Initiate your action plan.
7. Monitor the efficacy of your solutions.
8. Make midcourse corrections.

Sustainable landscape development will be increasingly popular with homeowners and landscape professionals because of these important contributions:

- **Direct economic payback.** Sustainability is good for profitability and property value because maintenance costs can be significantly reduced and any direct savings go directly to the property owner's pocket.
- **Environmental responsibility.** We all owe a debt to the world around us. By acting responsibly, we are more a *part of* the planet than *apart from* the planet.
- **Enhanced quality of life.** The quality of our lives is improved by sustainable practices. The air is cleaner, there is less noise pollution, and our surroundings reflect the aesthetic needs of humanity.

Perform an Environmental Audit of Your Property

The following questions will give you an opportunity to document the expenditures your property currently requires. After answering them, you will have a greater awareness of the impact that your landscape has on your pocketbook — and the earth.

Lawn Assessment

- What are the dimensions of your lawn (in square feet)? _____
  - Number of mowings per year _____
  - Cost per mowing $ _____
  - Total cost for lawn mowing per year (multiply two lines above) $ _____
- What are the dimensions (in linear feet) of the areas requiring edging? _____
  - Number of edging treatments done per year _____
  - Cost per edging treatment $ _____
  - Total cost $ _____
- What are the dimensions (in linear feet) of areas requiring trimming? _____
  - Number of trimming treatments done per year _____
  - Cost per trimming treatment $ _____
  - Total cost $ _____
- How many times do you fertilize your lawn in a year? _____
  - Cost per application $ _____
  - Total cost $ _____
- How many standard pesticide treatments do you apply to your lawn per year? _____
  - Cost per application $ _____
  - Total cost $ _____
- What are the dimensions (in square feet) of the lawn area you apply lime to? _____
  - How many lime applications in 10 years? _____
  - Cost per application $ _____
  - Total cost per 10 years $ _____
- How many square feet of lawn are compacted due to heavy foot traffic each year? _____
  - How many core aerations are done in 10 years? _____
  - Cost per core aeration $ _____
  - Total cost per 10 years $ _____

- What is the square footage of area you are likely to repair after winter damage? _____
  - Cost per year of lawn repair $ _____
- What is the average square footage of area watered during drought conditions each year? _____
  - Cost per year of waterings $ _____
- What is the square footage of area that is likely to be raked? _____
  - Cost per year of rakings $ _____
  - Total cost $ _____
- What is the square footage of lawn area under irrigation? _____
  - Gallons of water used annually _____
  - Cost per gallon $ _____
  - Total cost $ _____

Lawn maintenance cost summary

- Total of all annual costs $ _____
- Total square feet _____
- Cost per square foot $ _____
- Projected 10-year costs $ _____

Tree Assessment

- What is the direction of the prevailing winds? _____
  - Is the wind accelerated or funneled by any of the existing structures? (if so, indicate on plot plan) _____
- How many mature trees (> than 24" diameter) are there in high-people-activity areas? _____
- How many trees above 6" diameter but less than 24" diameter are there in high-people-activity areas? _____
- Are any of the existing trees indicating a hazardous situation? _____
- Are any of the existing trees showing signs of stress? _____
- What is the proximity of pine trees to lawn areas? _____

(continued on page 116)

- What is the proximity of salt-intolerant trees to walkways and road runoff? _____
- Are there any existing guys or stakes on the trees? _____

Shrub Assessment

- Are shrubs treated as individual plants or as massed arrangements? _____
- How many individual shrubs exist on the site? _____
- How many times a year are the shrubs trimmed? _____
- What is the cost of trimming annually? $ _____
- How many times a year are the shrubs fertilized? _____
- What is the cost of shrub fertilization annually? $ _____
- Are any of the shrubs given special protection for the winter? _____
- What is the square footage of shrub beds that is mulched? _____
- How much mulch is used annually? _____
  At what cost? $ _____

Herbaceous Plantings Assessment

- How many total square feet of herbaceous plantings are on the site? _____
- How many square feet are annuals (including vines)? _____
- How many square feet are perennials (including vines)? _____
- How many large bulbs (tulip, daffodil, hyacinth) are planted per year? _____
- How many bulbs are dug up and replanted per year? _____
- How much mulch is placed in these beds each year? _____
- What is the cost associated with this mulch enhancement? $ _____
- What is the annual cost for these planting beds for the following tasks?
  - Weeding $ _____
  - Edging $ _____
  - Deadheading $ _____
  - Thinning $ _____
  - Dividing $ _____
  - Staking $ _____
  - Fertilizing $ _____

Pest Control $ _____
Replanting $ _____
Irrigation $ _____
Total Costs $ _____

- What is the total annual cost of maintenance for shrubs and herbaceous planting beds on the site? _____
- What is the total square footage of all of these areas? _____
- What is the baseline cost of maintenance per square foot? $ _____
- What is the projected 10-year cumulative cost? $ _____
- What is the combined cost of lawn, shrubs, and herbaceous areas per annum? $ _____
- What is the projected 10-year cost for the same areas? 100-year? $ _____

General Audit Questions

- Are there any plant compatibility problems? _____
- Are there poor drainage areas? _____
- Is there an opportunity to use screening trees to reduce wind and subsequent energy demands? _____
- Is there an opportunity to reduce air-conditioning through the use of shade-producing trees or other plantings? _____
- Have there been outbreaks of insect or disease problems with plantings on the site? _____
- Is mowing and/or trimming difficult because of the configuration of the lawn in relation to site objects and access? _____
- Is safety compromised anywhere on the site because of landscape features? _____
- Is the landscape serving the human needs of the occupants? _____
- What are the recommendations of the maintenance contractors for improvements to the overall efficiency of their operations? _____
- What other issues were discovered in a survey of the property? _____

PART III

I Can't Do It All Myself
Hiring Landscape Contractors

10

Selecting Qualified Contractors

~

WHEN YOU'RE READY TO INVEST IN landscaping for your property, you're likely to be confronted with a wide array of contractors. These professionals all can play important roles in the creation, construction, and maintenance of that landscape. It has been our experience that many people are confused by the titles these tradespeople use. What is the difference between a landscape architect and a landscape designer? What areas of specialty do different landscape contractors provide?

We feel that using the services of landscape professionals is a wise course of action whether you are installing a large project like an entire yard or a small project such as a patio. When you employ a landscape professional you are assured of a level of quality in the finished product that most homeowners lack the time, tools, or expertise to produce.

Who's Who Among Landscaping Professionals?

To make sure you understand the different types of disciplines that are involved in the horticultural industry and its related fields, the following list will help to define the characteristics of each of these services.

Landscape Architect (ASLA)

Currently, forty-five states have laws that restrict the use of the title *landscape architect* to people who have attended and graduated from an accredited college or university. They also must have passed a national examination. Some states have an additional test by a state-regulated examining board. Apprenticeship with a registered landscape architect may also be required. Most landscape architects do not deal with residential projects. Nationally, only about twelve percent of these firms will deal with homeowners. Generally, the landscape architect's training emphasizes space design, civil engineering, and project management, rather than horticulture. As always, there can be notable exceptions to this general rule, but be sure that you consult chapter 12 for guidelines on asking the right questions when interviewing a potential landscape architect. (The letters *ASLA* usually designate a registered landscape architect who is a member of the American Society of Landscape Architects.)

Landscape Designer (LD)

No title laws restrict the use of the term *landscape designer*. Professional organizations do exist, however, that are attempting to set professional standards that will help consumers to identify qualified "LDs." The Association of Professional Landscape Designers is one such organization. (Certified members of this association use the designation *APLD* after their names.) A few schools grant degrees in landscape design, such as Radcliffe and Conway School of Design. Generally speaking, landscape designers are more familiar with plants and their cultural needs than are the landscape architects. They also are more likely to work on residential projects. They can be independent or be associated with a landscape construction firm.

Cooperative Extension Agent

The Cooperative Extension Service is a federally funded program that provides educational advice and training to the general public. One popular educational service is the Master Gardener Program. Members of this program receive broad training in the field of horticulture. Extension agents are usually associated with a major university in the state. In most states where agriculture is important, each county usually has an extension agent representing the public's needs. Another federally run program, once known as the Soil Conservation Service (SCS), was recently changed to the Natural Resource Conservation Service (NRCS). This service is used primarily by farmers and other agricultural concerns.

Nursery Professional

Experience is one of the best teachers of the growing of plants. Because of this, nurserypeople can be one of your most valuable plant information resources. Garden centers and retail nurseries are the places you find these professionals. Many nurserypeople have bachelor's degrees in horticulture and are members of state and national professional organizations. Look to certified nursery professionals for the best advice on plants. However, just because someone works at a garden center does not necessarily mean that he or she is qualified. You may be dealing with someone who waters the plants on the weekend as a part-time employee. By using our questions in chapter 12 you will soon be able to ascertain the difference.

Arborist

An arborist has demonstrated a working knowledge of tree care and maintenance. Some states require that an arborist be licensed and insured in order to do tree work. Typical activities carried out by arborists are pruning, felling, cabling, bracing, fertilizing, spraying, stump grinding, and consulting. There are two types of arborist: consulting and working. A consulting arborist (CA) offers specialized information, such as providing a monetary basis for value on your trees or identifying potentially hazardous conditions. Before hiring a working arborist for the spraying of your trees, be sure that he or she is properly licensed for applying chemicals.

Lawn-Care and Spray Specialist

There are numerous lawn-care companies that help homes and businesses maintain a lush, insect- and weed-free lawn. Some specialize in an organic approach using the latest IPM (Integrated Pest Management) techniques. Others have regularly scheduled sprays that take care of a wide variety of lawn problems. Be sure that the company is properly licensed for the application of chemicals and follows all of the statutes dictated by your local and state regulatory agencies.

Horticulturalist

Horticulturalists have a great deal of experience with plants in general and often have degrees in horticulture or plant science. They are often hired by landscape companies, greenhouses, nurseries, or garden centers.

Landscape Broker

The "broker" is defined as a go-between or an agent who could be working for either the homeowner or the landscape professional. He or she should be extremely knowledgeable about all aspects of the landscape construction process. Brokers usually specialize in either plant brokerage or contract brokerage. Plant brokers

have good connections with many growers and plant suppliers. Contract brokers help to negotiate contracts and administer work that is performed. They can be paid hourly or work on a percentage-fee basis, depending on who they are working for or the type of work.

Consultant

A consultant is sometimes referred to as an "expert." Experts have been defined as those who have no doubt in their minds about a given subject. They might be wrong, but they have no doubt in their minds! The point here is that there is always more to know about any subject. Therefore, understand that a consultant may not always be able to address your needs. All of the professionals listed here can act in the role of consultant. You do not need to have a degree to have an opinion. The professional consultant, however, does need to know your subject thoroughly. It never hurts to get a second opinion from another qualified consultant.

Forester

You would hire a forester for dealing with woodlots and their management. Foresters can advise on timber quality or pulpwood value. They will be able to mark trees in woods you own for selective thinning or harvesting. To improve the future value of a woodlot, a forester should be consulted for developing a timber stand improvement (TSI) plan. This plan will help to provide a continuous yield of firewood and other forest products. Usually a forester has attended a college accredited in forestry and has received at the very least an associate's degree in forest technology.

Site Contractor

A site contractor is primarily focused on excavation. These contractors specialize in grading, digging, filling, and drainage, and work on roads, drainage ditches, driveways, foundations, and septic systems. They also have the greatest opportunity to damage existing trees. Their heavy equipment can easily drip oil and hydraulic fluid, compact soils, scrape bark, and break branches (see chapter 4 for ways to prevent this).

Landscape Contractor

The term *landscaper* or *landscape contractor* has created a great deal of misunderstanding. Various contractors provide different services and specialties. Be sure that the company you choose has the expertise for your specific project.

The two types of landscape contractors are construction and maintenance. Occasionally a company does both; in that case you need to be sure that the crew working on your property is familiar with construction and is not simply a maintenance crew. (Make sure as well that a residential construction crew is installing your landscape and not a commercial construction crew.)

While construction contractors are trained primarily in the installation of various landscaping components, maintenance contractors focus on caring for landscaping once it's in place. They have special licenses for pest control because of the application of chemical pesticides. You will want them to be experienced in lawn-mowing practices that will promote a healthy lawn environment, and to be familiar with routine herbaceous maintenance as well as woody shrub care.

Related Professionals

In the course of landscape construction, you may need the services of a number of other professionals. The following list should give you an idea of who you might have to deal with. If

---

SPECIALTY AREAS FOR RESIDENTIAL CONSTRUCTION CONTRACTORS

Not all landscape contractors are equally familiar with all of these areas. It is important that you ask the right questions to ensure you are getting someone with the knowledge and skills for your job (see chapter 12).

Lawn installation/seeding
Timber work
Carpentry
Fencing
Flat masonry (patios, walks, paths)
Planting
Stone walls
Water gardens
Irrigation
Lighting

SERVICES PROVIDED BY A LANDSCAPE MAINTENANCE CONTRACTOR

Spraying
Mowing
Pruning
Bed maintenance: fertilization, weeding, edging, root division

---

the landscape contractor is acting as a general contractor (GC) on your job, he or she will contract out for these services.

- Electrician
- Entomologist/pathologist
- Geologist
- Mason
- Plumber
- Surveyor

Criteria for Selecting a Landscape Professional

Now that you have a good idea of what types of services you can expect from different types of contractors, you should also be aware of what else you need to know in making your selection. Following are the steps for an initial review of a professional's qualifications.

1. Ask to see a portfolio. Landscape contractors or designers should be proud of their work. They should offer to show you pictures without being asked. When you're looking at their pictures, pay particular attention to the ones that are similar to your situation. It's not a good idea to hire someone if you have a difficult project and he or she has no experience. Pictures are worth a thousand words.

2. Ask how long they've been in business. This question is not asked frequently enough of prospective contractors. We've seen too many jobs "go bad" because expectations weren't met, many times due to the contractor's lack of experience. Don't hire someone who is learning on your project. Even though the price may be lower than that of a more experienced contractor, there is a good reason for that. If the inexperienced person does not know the difficulty involved in the project, you won't get an accurate pricing. Also, you may end up with a half-finished project with no one to complete it, or an incorrectly installed project that is now a liability. If you have a technically complicated project, you should be particularly leery of offering it to an inexperienced contractor. In this case, the low price wouldn't be your best price. Not only are you likely to be unhappy with the results, but in some cases you also could have a liability problem. For example, if a retaining wall suddenly lets go because of improper construction and destroys a car or, even worse, injures someone, you could have a lawsuit on your hands. For many aspects of landscape construction, a high level of expertise and experience is required for correct installation. Selecting the *right* contractor for the job is imperative.

3. Ask for references and check them. We always ask our clients to fill out an evaluation sheet on each project we complete. We feel it's important that the people we've worked for have an opportunity to evaluate our performance. These sheets are made into a reference list for our new and prospective customers. This system does two things for us. First, it gives the public a chance to check up on us to ensure that we're representing ourselves accurately. Second, it keeps us mindful of our responsibility to the client to provide a quality product. If the company you're considering doesn't have this attitude, look for another company.

4. Ask for a list of credentials and licenses. Because landscaping is an easy-entrance business, the public should be leery of charlatans in this industry. There are people doing business as landscapers who are more appropriately called "landscrapers." All they need to start a landscaping business is a truck and a few tools. Recently, we've seen other landscaper look-alikes that make the "landscraper" seem like a professional. These folks don't even have a truck and are known in the trade as "trunkslammers." They throw a few tools into the car and they're in business.

There is no law that requires landscapers to be professionally certified, even though doing the job effectively requires a great deal of knowledge and skill. Most professional organizations encourage some type of certification program within their own ranks. Performance of certain landscaping practices may be legally required to be done by properly licensed and certified individuals. For example, in the state of Maine you need to be licensed to apply pesticides or perform any tree work. These requirements look out for the best interests of the general public. Don't be afraid to ask for a list of your prospective contractor's credentials. This helps you to be confident in his or her ability to provide you with a quality service.

5. Ask to see work in the event the contractor doesn't have a portfolio. Ask to see prospective contractors' work firsthand. This makes it easier for you to visualize what your project might look like when complete. If a contractor directs you to a job that he says he has installed, confirm it with the owner of the property. It is easy to steal someone else's work just by showing it and claiming to have done it. Don't be fooled by this.

6. Ask to see proof of insurance. The need for insurance can't be stressed enough. It keeps customers confident in their security from accidents. It also protects consumers from unscrupulous contractors. Without proper protection, you might be inviting a lawsuit into your yard. Ask to see proof of insurance!

CERTIFICATIONS TO LOOK FOR IN YOUR CONTRACTORS

- Certified Pesticide Applicator
- Certified Arborist
- Certified Nurseryman
- Certified Landscape Professional (CLP)
- Professional Landscape Designer (PLD)
- Landscape Architect (ASLA) (American Society of Landscape Architects)
- Member, ALCA (Association of Landscape Contractors of America)
- Member, AAN (American Association of Nurserymen)
- Member, NAA (National Arborist Association)
- Member, PGMS (Professional Grounds Management Society)
- Member, PLCAA (Professional Lawn Care Applicators Association)
- Member, ISA (International Society of Arboriculture)

---

7. Ask about their guarantee. Guarantees for landscape construction range from nothing to everything. A good company will stand behind its hardscape construction one hundred percent. Guarantees for softscape, or the living part of the landscape, are more tenuous because of the variables involved. A good guarantee is one hundred percent satisfaction during the growing season of the installation. Replacement of plants that die during the winter often results in a sharing of the replacement cost. For instance, the landscaper might cover the cost of the plant, and the homeowner might pay for the labor. Beware of contractors who promise you the moon. It's not practical to expect to get a plant replaced for free after a harsh winter that no one can control. In some cases, a larger company may give a full one- or two-year guarantee on its plantings. This doesn't mean you *can't* trust it. Regardless of the guarantee, be aware that the potential costs of replacements have been factored into what are likely to be higher planting costs.

8. Be sure you like the contractor and feel you will work well together. If you're doing a landscape project at your home, the last thing that you want is someone who's around day after day you don't like. This adds stress to your life and could affect the quality of workmanship provided by the contractor. Be aware of how you're feeling toward the people conducting the sales meeting and what their attitude is toward you. You should feel that your concerns are important, that you are very important, and that you'll like working with them.

A larger landscape company typically has a salesperson who makes the initial contact. Then you may talk to, and work with, the designer. In some cases this may be the same person. After your design is complete, you should receive a proposal giving the prices for the project. A typical contract spells out the guarantee, prices, work to be done, and payment schedule. Don't allow someone to work at your home without a written and signed contract that includes these details. After you have signed the contract, the company's project coordinator will take over. This person is in charge of purchasing the materials needed for the job and is responsible for developing the strategy and timetable for your work. He or she is the company's link between you and the job foreman, who is in charge of all the construction on the site. The project coordinator is your immediate sounding board for questions and problems that can arise throughout the course of the work.

If you're working with a smaller company, it's possible that one person will be the project coordinator and the job foreman. Other companies use the designer as the project coordinator and the job foreman for added continuity. In any case, be sure that you hire professionals with an established track record who will most likely be there year after year to take care of your long-term needs.

Even in the best-planned project, unexpected situations will arise. You need to be able to talk with each other and work out problems.

SPECIAL NOTE ABOUT CONTRACTOR INTERVIEWS

Be sure to inquire about Material Safety Data Sheets, and ask to review them. The contractor is required by law to have MSDS available for review. If the contractor is using chemicals or any other material that is deemed to be hazardous, the MSDS must be on hand.

Other Choices for Contracting Services

Another way to choose a contractor is through the bidding process. You, the owner, invite two or three companies to bid on your project. This is a fair process that can help you to determine that you are getting the best market price. It is imperative that the contractors who are bidding on your project all have the same information presented in the same way. If your landscape construction job is a large or complex one, you should use a landscape architect or designer to prepare the specification documents and drawing information. It is his or her job to make sure that all the information is the same. The biggest drawback to this option is the expense of design and specification writing; but if your job is complicated, it is the best way to get a quality design and installation.

Another choice is to use the services of a company that handles both design and construction, called a design/build company. These companies are a good buy since they have an architect or designer on staff, so design and construction specifications are an in-house standard, and you won't need another firm to draw up specifications for the bidding process. In other words, if a stone retaining wall is part of the design, it is expected that the firm knows how to build that wall and does not need specifications drawn up. For this reason, the design process is less expensive, but it also means you must be very sure of the reputation and experience of the firm.

11

Negotiating Contracts

~

I T IS ALWAYS A GOOD IDEA TO HAVE A CONTRACT with your contractor, no matter how large or small the job. Most of these contracts are derived from a standard form. Each contract should have certain key elements.

A contract is in essence a summation of communications between two parties. A good contractor will be able to write a contract that clearly delineates his or her intentions. As the homeowner, you are responsible for communicating your needs and wishes. Jobs with a high level of satisfaction are jobs where expectations were clearly stated. Problems arise when you are expecting one thing and you get another (of lower quality). Quality is not defined by the contract or the contractor — it is defined by the customer's expectations. If you do not know what to expect, look to the contractor to give you some direction or guidelines; ask the questions detailed in the next chapter.

In looking at any contract, it is important to use your common sense. Both parties' interests and rights should be well represented in a good contract. The contractor should be assured of maintaining a positive cash flow and that he or she is not expected to do unreasonable tasks. The homeowner should be assured that work will be done on time, correctly, and without unreasonable cost overruns. It is extremely important to read the contract carefully before you sign it.

The Contents of a Contract

To start with, your name, address, and phone number, as well as the contractor's name, address, and phone number should be on any contract you sign. A description of the project is also very important. There needs to be a clear understanding of the work to be done. However, every single detail does not need to be itemized. For example, suppose you have already worked with a particular landscape design/build firm, or have a recommendation from a friend. You know the company does a great perennial garden, but you do not know much about these types of flowers. In that case, you may want just a description of the square footage and the number of plants they plan to use, and then trust the contractor's judgment for the correct selections. In these sorts of cases it is understandable that you may not have every detail spelled out in a contract.

Description of Project

It is important in all contracts to have a definitive explanation of the size of the project. For instance, make sure you know how long and high a stone wall is supposed to be, and what kind of stone will be used. If the contract simply states "Stone Wall," you have no legal recourse if the wall is six inches high and five feet long and you were expecting it to be two feet high and twenty feet long. If there is a separate description or drawing, the contract should refer to it with specific identification.

It is essential that you have a clear understanding of what you expect from the contractor and that the contractor is fully aware of your expectations. Make sure, for example, that you

understand the layout of the patio. Check out the type of mulch to be used and have it in writing. Specify flower color. Mention the sizes of the plants. Determine when the work will start. In other words, be sure to state what is important to you and what you want no confusion about.

Statement of Guarantee

The next thing you should look for is a statement of the guarantee. This will vary widely, depending on the type of work you are having done. Many states mandate a one-year guarantee time period for workmanship. Of course, you should always check your own state's statutes. Contact the local state representative for your district and he or she will gladly assist you. It is fairly standard in the landscape industry to expect plant material to be guaranteed for a full growing season or one year. This is usually contingent on your care of the plants, and there are exceptions for such things as vandalism and what are known as "Acts of God," such as floods, tornadoes, earthquakes, and droughts. Regardless, you should always be aware of care instructions for the landscape, which should be provided by your contractor. This way you will know how much to water, when to fertilize, and how much and when to prune.

Terms of Payment

The payment terms are very important as well. You should know exactly how much the project will cost and when payments are due. Never pay in full before the project has been completed. This is another reason why you need to make sure you understand exactly what the finished project should include. You need to be very clear about these points!

Many firms will ask for a deposit. This could range from ten percent of the cost of the project to half, and varies according to the amount of materials to be used as well as their relative costs. In order for contractors to be able to pay suppliers, they need this deposit before, or when, the job starts.

Sometimes, especially if it is a fairly sizable project, you may arrange to make payments over the course of the project as tasks are accomplished and materials arrive on site. This is frequently how commercial jobs are paid. Usually you have from ten to thirty days to pay the final amount. If you are satisfied with the job that has been performed, be sure to pay your bill on time. Because of the seasonal nature of the landscape business, cash flow can be a problem for landscapers.

Terms for Extra Add-On Costs

The contract should also include something about extras. Most jobs will have opportunities for you to save some money by adding to the scope of work. For example, you realize that while the landscape people are planting the two maples, you could have them plant an apple tree you wanted, but for some reason you had overlooked that possibility in the original contract.

YOUR RIGHTS AS A CONSUMER

As the consumer of a service, you have certain rights. Some of these rights vary from state to state, but there are some universal rights. You always have the option of small claims court or a lawsuit. These, however, should be a last resort — it can be expensive to sue, and there is no guarantee that you will win all damages.

Another problem might be that the contractor has no money and could file for bankruptcy protection as a result of your lawsuit. In small claims court you can represent yourself to lower your costs and even win your claim. There is no guarantee, however, that you will ever collect. In fact, this is often the case. All you win is the judgment and not the award of money or compensation.

This actually happens quite frequently. You say, "While you're at the nursery please pick up this apple tree and plant it here."

You should ask for an add-on card or a change-order slip to be made out; make sure a copy is given to you. The information on the card can be as simple as the cost of the tree, the cost for planting, and the total. You should sign it and so should the contractor or the contractor's foreman. This way you both know the extra cost. Even if there are several add-ons during the course of the job, you will not have any surprises. This method also keeps the contractor accountable for the work he or she has performed.

Work Schedule

Since scheduling is an important component of your job, you may want to include some provision in your contract to address a reasonable time limit for completion. Landscape people are especially subject to weather delays, so it is a good idea to have some latitude in this provision. The contract should state that the work will be completed in "X" number of days, weather permitting. This ensures that once the job begins, people will be on site performing their work (weather permitting). This way you won't have a contractor start the job one day, then leave your yard torn up for five days and come back on the sixth, and then leave again, etc.

Unforeseen Circumstances

Contracts also usually include a clause about unforeseen hazards or unusual conditions, also known as "concealed contingencies," which may involve extra costs. For example, during excavation, rock ledge is discovered under six inches of soil in the place where you have contracted to have a tree planted. You did not know the ledge was there when you entered into the agreement, and since the job contracted for appeared to be simple, you did not pay to have a geological survey done. No one knew the problem existed. This situation would warrant a change in the price because the scope of work has changed. If a hole for the tree has to be jackhammered, this creates an extra expense through no fault of the contractor. This is, of course, an extreme measure, and moving the location of the tree may be easier. However, moving the tree may not be possible, if the lot is too small or the ledge is too extensive, and the extra cost is warranted.

Without such a clause the contractor generally would bear the cost of such changes. With this clause, the contractor does not have to carry a large contingency lump of money in his or her contract with you to cover unforeseen problems. This makes for a more cost-effective job for you, as the consumer.

Addressing Potential Problems

In essence, a contract is a "risk allocation document." It is intended to detail who is responsible for certain aspects of work, what that work is, who is responsible for payment, when it is due, who is responsible for unforeseen changes, and who bears the responsibility if mistakes happen. When both parties sign a statement of this understanding, it demonstrates that there is an agreement and that all of the terms are acceptable.

Even with all of these items covered in the contract there are provisions that are implied, but may not exist in so many words. For example, it is expected that work will be carried out in a workmanlike fashion and will be exemplary of industry standards. When the contractor has plans and specifications supplied by the owner, there is an assumption that those plans and specifications are accurate and representative of the work to be performed. They

should also meet industry standards. If the plans prove to be faulty, the contractor is not liable for the damages. The "Spearin Doctrine" (a precedent-setting case) states that since the owner is responsible for accurate plans, any warranty on the work that is performed is contingent upon plans that meet the terms laid out in the signed contract.

It can't be overstated how important it is that you, the homeowner, are sure that the plans are accurate and will meet your expectations. It is also extremely important that you choose a designer, architect, landscape contractor, or design/build firm with a good track record. A reputable company is likely to point out deficiencies in a plan or blueprint before the signing of a contract.

Using a Mediator

As the property owner, you have one very important right — to stop the work if you feel that it is unsatisfactory. If there is a major problem and you can't resolve the issue, you may want to consult with an objective third party or enter into a nonbinding mediation. Your mediator should have impeccable credentials and should not be in any way self-served in settling the dispute other than to be paid a fee for consultation. The National Construction Industry Arbitration Committee along with the American Arbitration Association has set up rules for mediation. Under these guidelines the AAA will provide mediators who can help resolve a dispute.

Occasionally, you may need an expert to resolve questions that arise in the execution of the contract. A variety of resources can provide answers. For example, the horticulture department of a college can be a good source for plant experts. Professional groups or organizations of retired individuals may be helpful. Trade organizations such as the Masons are another good source for locating tradespeople.

This route should help you avoid costly lawsuits and to continue your job. It should also be noted that in these cases there is rarely one party who is all wrong or all right. As with most situations, there are two sides to the story. Mediation should help lead to a compromise that will complete the job and serve everyone's needs. Sometimes the solution lies in understanding that the two opposing parties are on one team. The resolution of the problems and issues can end in a win/win situation.

Terminating a Contract

If all efforts to make the job go well have failed and there is no other recourse, you can terminate the contract. This can be done by either party and the contract language should have something about the terms of "default" in it. Terminating the contract could happen because you are not happy with the quality of work or materials, or because the contractor is unhappy with the payments. This is unusual in residential landscape construction, but is a remote possibility. Check with your lawyer before you make such a move to see what sort of financial obligations you might incur.

Remember, people are fallible and make mistakes. If you have chosen your contractor well, he or she should be willing to fix any problems. Informal resolution to disputes is generally the best situation for everybody. Make sure that the management of the company you are working with is aware of any problem or situation that may jeopardize the successful completion of your job. Be sure to talk to the person who has the authority to resolve the dispute.

12

Asking the Right Questions
of Contractors

THIS CHAPTER LOOKS AT THE POSSIBLE pitfalls that may cause problems if you don't ask the right questions. By asking the right questions of the right person at the right time, you will avoid many costly errors. These questions need to be asked regardless of whether you are a do-it-yourselfer or you are working with a landscape professional. Typically, problems occur because of the following:

■ Poor planning
■ Improper construction sequence
■ Lack of understanding of drainage, hardscape elements, plant growth forms and habits, aesthetic principles, or the true purpose of the landscape elements

In this chapter, we try to help you anticipate what can go wrong in these areas and offer guidance on how to avoid problems before they arise, by asking questions and informing yourself about what is going on in your landscaping construction.

Basic Questions to Ask in the Planning Stages

Proper planning is essential to save yourself time and money. If you do not plan ahead, you may end up with significant additions to your anticipated project costs. This may mean that your budget will be shot to pieces and you will be unable to complete your landscape project. Some of the most important questions you need to ask in this regard will be asked of yourself. These questions will fall into two categories: *wants* and *needs.*

"Needs" are things that you can't do without. In the case of a house, your needs are walls, doors, windows, floors, etc. In a landscape your needs are walkways, driveways, drainage, plants, etc. "Wants" are things that you would like to have but are not essential. For a a house, wants might be a dishwasher, fireplace, Jacuzzi, certain style of architecture, skylight, etc. Wants for your landscape might include a swimming pool, a reading nook, a gazebo, an herb garden, an orchard, etc.

Chapter 6 gives you a complete overview of the questions you should be asking at this stage to delineate your wants and needs.

Drainage Issues

Drainage is one of your first concerns. You should never begin any landscape work until all issues of drainage have been adequately addressed. Many problems arise because of improper drainage, including:

- Flooded basements
- Water pooling in lawns, driveways, walks, patios, etc.
- Erosion on slopes
- Downspout and roof valley erosion, undermining of driveways, retaining walls, and other structures
- Ice dams
- Frost heaving of driveways, walls, and walks
- Landslides and mudslides
- Slumps and sinkholes
- Root rot on trees

All of these conditions can not only reduce the inherent value of your property, but they can also significantly reduce the money you have in the bank.

Questions to ask your contractor:

1. How do I resolve my problem with _____ ? (see list at left below)

2. Do you anticipate I will have any other drainage problems?

3. How deep will you dig the drip edge? The drip edge must be at least six inches deep.

4. What type of edging will you use? Remember that a drip edge without edging will be a maintenance problem — grass or other ground covers will grow into this area readily.

5. Are you using a level to determine proper slope of drainage? The answer should be yes, because a minimum of a quarter-inch drop per linear foot of pipe is necessary for positive drainage. This is too small to be done accurately by eye.

6. Do you plan to use solid or perforated pipe? Solid pipe moves water from one point to the other quickly if pitched properly. Perforated pipe picks up water and disperses it along the way.

7. What have you done to keep sand from clogging the pipe? If there is no filtering system in place, the pipes may fill with sand and cease to function as effective drains.

Construction Sequence

What is the most cost-effective construction sequence to follow? Building a landscape requires a certain order of installation. This is true for the home installation as well as the professionally installed landscape. Many times, homeowners can't afford to install the entire landscape at once. In this case, there are many approaches to installation based on the needs of the site or the owner. If having established plants is very important to you, then plant all your trees the first year, shrubs the second year, ground cover in the third year, and finally build the deck on the back of the house. However, if the deck is more important to you, build it first. Of course, the premise of this is that you are not restricting access to the back of the house by the planting of trees and shrubs. You do not want to "paint yourself into a corner" by eliminating your access to any portion of the yard. If the site is open, you have more options.

Generally speaking, though, if you can afford to install the entire landscape at one time, this is the best idea. Considerable money can be saved because the sequence of installation is not broken. In other words, you don't have to rip up a completed portion of the landscape to access the next phase of construction.

For example, stone walls should be one of the first construction projects because the wall will require a backhoe for excavation and the hauling of heavy stones. It would be unfortunate and costly to have put in a lawn or garden the year before and then have to tear it up for the installation of a wall. Sometimes this scenario is unavoidable, but of course it's best not to have to go backward to go forward.

One of the other firsts in your construction sequence should be the planting of large trees. Large trees require machinery to plant and cause the same type of disturbance as putting in a wall. If you try to plant a very heavy tree without equipment, it can be harmful to the tree's health. This is because the rootball may get crushed if it is rolled into place rather than set. This creates air pockets and rips moisture-gathering root hairs from the root stems.

The next step may be the installation of a patio and walkways. This construction may require a backhoe as well. It will definitely require heavy materials such as crushed stone or gravel and a surface material such as brick, stone, or concrete paver.

Bed preparation should also be done early. This work is done the most cost effectively by a backhoe with a front-loading bucket. While digging out areas for the beds, also excavate water gardens and trenches for electrical conduit or irrigation pipes. Planting of shrubs and flowers is the next logical step. Hand tools are generally all that is needed for correct planting. Mulch, however, may be transported via tractor bucket to speed this portion of planting.

It is not until this point that you should be spreading loam for the lawn. Large lawns may require a bulldozer for the most cost-effective way to grade and spread the loam. This is also the time to put in an irrigation system if you need one, since at this point the loam has been roughly spread but the fine-grading of the lawn area has not been done.

Additions to the landscape — garden sheds, gazebos, or 12-volt lighting — can be added later, but again, if funds allow, any part of the construction that requires large equipment should be done before the last step, which is the fine-grading, raking, and seeding of the yard.

Questions to Ask About Hardscaping Elements

Hardscape is the part of your yard made up of landscape elements that are not plants. Structures, walls, fences, walkways, and irrigation are all examples of hardscape elements. Questions about this essential aspect of your exterior decorating are categorized here according to each specific element.

Walls

1. What kind of soils will the wall be built on? The type of soil will affect the amount of drainage necessary. Heavy or silty types of soil will require a more elaborate system than a well-draining sandy soil. Be sure your contractor is aware of the soil type so that you will get an accurate proposal and avoid any cost surprises.

2. Is the base sufficient for this site considering the existing soil type and amount of frost in this region? In cold regions with frost heaving, it is important to have good drainage under a dry-laid wall and behind a dry-laid retaining wall. Be sure your contractor has experience in this type of wall construction in your area; make sure the walls he or she has built locally are still standing after several winters. In warm areas where frost is not an issue, you can choose a wet-laid wall without fear of damage. In both cases, good drainage is essential, because hydraulic pressure can and will push a wall over regardless of the presence of frost. Frost will just accelerate the process.

3. What are the price differences for types of stone? There are two basic ways of acquiring stone. Quarried stone can be bought through many aggregate supply businesses, which sell sand, gravel, loam, and loose stone. Fieldstone can be purchased from farms where walls are being taken down. Some businesses harvest stone for sale. Granite quarries also occasionally make wall stone available to the consumer.

4. Do you plan on building this wall as dry laid or wet laid? A dry-laid wall is constructed without concrete; a wet-laid wall with concrete. In a region of significant freezing and thawing, a wet-laid stone wall is generally not recommended.

5. If wet laid, how deep is the base you plan to build? In a frost zone, for the best results, the base should be as deep as the average frost line. In parts of New England, that can be more than five feet. This base could be made of a material that drains well, such as crushed gravel or stone, or it could be made of concrete.

6. Do you plan on using geotextile fabric, crushed stone, and perforated pipe behind my retaining wall? We recommend the use of these for drainage behind every retaining wall more than two feet high. Any retaining wall, regardless of height, should have a geotextile fabric behind it. This filter fabric allows water to pass through it, but keeps the soil in place behind the wall. If you do not use filter fabric, soils may eventually be washed through the wall, which creates pockets and undermining behind the wall. This may eventually cause it to collapse or cause slumping of the soil behind the wall.

Walkways, Paths, Terraces, and Patios

1. What kind of base do you intend on using to prevent frost heaving and to promote good drainage? If you want paths or patios on land with clay or claylike conditions where water does not percolate quickly, you need to install some type of drainage system, which may include piping to take water away from under the paved area. If you simply place draining material in such an area, the water will accumulate as if in a swimming pool, and will cause severe heaving damage from frost. In all cases, a good draining material such as crushed stone should be used as a component of your base. It should also be compacted correctly to minimize heaving; we recommend using a gas-driven plate compactor, in depths of no more than four inches at one time.

2. Will the paving material (brick, concrete, cement paver, fieldstone, etc.) stand up to the elements? All these materials are appropriate for paving. Used clay bricks or concrete paver can be less expensive, but be careful if you use reclaimed bricks or concrete products — they are more susceptible to water absorption and are more likely to break apart in freezing conditions. We suggest dipping in a waterproofing substance to help prolong the life of your paving.

3. What can I do to prolong the life of my paving material? Several companies manufacture water sealants, which help to prolong the life of your masonry. When buying clay bricks, be sure that you are purchasing the densest brick possible. Porous bricks have openings that allow the penetration of water. They will tend to break apart if you live in an area that is prone to freezing.

4. How expensive will repair work be, if necessary? We recommend the dry-laid method because of its comparatively low cost of repairs. If you decide to use concrete in your patio, walls, or walks, you can expect that any repair will be more expensive. Repairs are usually very noticeable with concrete because it is hard to match color and texture. This is not to say that concrete can't be used outside or that it is necessarily the most expensive, but its use is determined by local conditions and circumstances. Be sure that the contractor has experience in using concrete. Ask to see examples of his or her oldest exterior work.

Lighting

1. Is 12-volt lighting something you carry? Twelve-volt lighting is an increasingly popular alternative for outdoor landscape illumination.

2. Is 12-volt lighting appropriate for my yard? Twelve-volt lighting systems are generally appropriate for any residential setting.

3. Will you be using a licensed electrician to install any 120-volt systems? Because of the potential for electrocution, a 120-volt system should be installed by a licensed electrician who is aware of local building codes and knows how to handle exterior installations.

4. Do you have a variety of lines of 12-volt systems? There are many 12-volt systems to choose from. Nurseries and hardware stores are good places to look.

5. If a 120-volt system is used outside, is the wire placed in conduit and does it meet local code? Outdoor installation of 120-volt lines often requires conduit placed at specific depths. Warning flagging in the soil just above the conduit is also usually required.

Fences

1. What kind of wood are you using for the posts? There are several good choices for fence posts, including cedar, black locust, sassafras, and pressure-treated pine or hemlock.

2. Are you planning to paint or stain this fence to make it last longer? If you are using a rot-resistant wood, such as cedar or black locust, it is not necessary to paint or stain. It may be an aesthetic or design issue. For example, if you want a classic white picket fence, you have to paint the wood white. You can save money, however, by using pine for the pickets and rot-resistant wood for the posts and cross members.

3. What can I do to prevent the "checking" of the wood in my fence? As the wood dries out, it will split and crack on the end of the board. This is referred to as checking. By maintaining the natural oils and moisture of the wood, you can reduce the degree to which checking occurs. Stains, oils, and paints can help to reduce the effects of drying.

4. Will you be treating the posts with creosote? We don't recommend creosote, because it can poison the roots of some plants. It is a restricted substance and can't be purchased without special permission.

Water Gardens

1. What is the thickness and what type of liner do you plan on using? Anywhere from twenty to forty mil is a good thickness to use for free-forming liners. (A mil is .001 of an inch.) Although forty-mil is more expensive, it may well be worth the extra money because it lasts longer.

2. Will you be using an electrician to do the wiring? As mentioned above, if you are going to use a 120-volt system, it must be installed by a licensed electrician knowledgeable about local building codes and exterior installations.

3. If you use a vinyl liner, are you preparing the base around the pool so no stones can cut the vinyl in the future? You should always have a four- to five-inch-thick layer of sand as a buffer zone between the existing subsoil and the liner. Without this buffer, undetected sharp stones or building debris may cause a puncture.

4. Are low-voltage lighting and pumps a possibility for the pool? Low-voltage lights are very attractive and practical for your water garden. Pumps for circulating water are usually 120 volt. The pump size determines how much water circulates per hour.

5. Do you plan on using plants in the garden? If so, what kind of maintenance will they need? Water lilies, duck potatoes, water locust, and a wide array of other water-loving plants will make your water garden an enchanting place — and will also require some maintenance. Be sure to get a full explanation of the plants' maintenance needs before you purchase.

6. Is there a way to empty the pool for cleanup? This is an essential component of the well-designed water garden. You can simply use the pump in place for the garden's circulation or have a sump pump handy.

7. Do you anticipate a problem with overhead leaf fall? Be sure to locate your water feature away from large-leaved deciduous trees. Trees such as maple or oak can be a terrible nuisance in the fall.

Irrigation

One of the most important questions you need to ask is whether you need an irrigation system to begin with. Many areas of the country have severe shortages of water or are instituting watering bans. In some cases, irrigation will be an essential component for the well-being of the landscape, but you may want to consider plant choices that require less water. This type of landscape approach is known as "xeriscaping," and is becoming popular in arid climates. If you do plan to install an extensive system, you need to be careful of mature trees in the landscape. Take care not to cut too many support and feeder roots of these trees. Another cause for concern is what is known as "changed water conditions." The existing trees have become accustomed to a certain amount of water. If you add water to certain soils by irrigation, you may be causing rotting at the root level and endangering the tree's health as well as your own safety — the tree could uproot and fall over.

1. Do you have a design for the system? The company installing the irrigation for you should have no trouble putting together a diagram for the layout of the proposed system. This design enables it to put together a good estimate and to place watering heads effectively.

2. How much maintenance will this system require each year? Typically, an irrigation system needs maintenance only twice a year — at the beginning and the end of the growing season.

3. How much water will the system use? You will want to regulate the volume of water as the seasons dictate. For example, if your region has extensive rains in the spring, you will not need to operate the system. The control panel of your irrigation system allows you to respond to the vagaries of the weather. Some systems have a monitor in the soil that turns the system on automatically when the ground becomes dry.

4. Do you maintain, open, and close these systems?

5. If not, who does?

6. When the power goes off, will I have to reprogram the watering schedule? You should look for a system with a battery backup.

7. Where will we put the control board? The board should be easily accessible and kept out of the weather. Ideally, you should be able to program it and see it running from the same location.

8. How do you reprogram the control board? Before the contractor finishes, be sure you have a written step-by-step procedure to follow if the system shuts down. This should include the phone number of the person or company that installed the system.

Structures

1. What kind of woods do you plan to use? You should be using rot-resistant woods for the floor and wall supports. Consider the use of concrete for the foundation. If you are in a termite-prone climate, you want to make sure that there is sufficient space between the ground and the wood portion of your structure. The purpose and desired finished appearance of the structure will help to determine the wood that you choose.

2. What kind of maintenance can I expect? Most wood structures require about the same type and level of maintenance. However, something unusual, such as a ramada with a thatch roof, can require considerably more maintenance than an asphalt shingle roof.

3. Is it big enough for my present and future needs? Try to think ahead. Are you going to have more children, is a relative coming to live with you? By answering these questions you are more apt to consider future needs.

4. Will you be using a stain or paint? If you are using a rot-resistant wood, such as cedar or black locust, it is not necessary to paint or stain. It may be an aesthetic or design issue or you may want to match surrounding structures such as your house, garage, or barn.

5. What is the normal life of a structure of this nature? If you are using concrete or stone foundations and rot-resistant wood, and

you provide a regular maintenance regimen, your structure should last for generations. However, a pole structure (such as cedar posts for a grape arbor or pergola) will last twenty to thirty years.

Miscellaneous Hardscape Items

1. Do you have any suggestions for detail items to finish off my landscape? Landscape sculpture and artifacts range from the ridiculous to the sublime. Although you may like a particular style of ornamentation, you need to consider the impact that it will have on the perceived value of your property. If you are planning to sell the house, this is particularly important to consider. Some examples of standard ornaments you may want to add that may or may not suit the tastes of potential buyers are flagpoles, hitching posts, granite mailbox posts, sundials, hammocks, benches, millstones, lions, reflecting balls, concrete deer, Japanese lanterns, boulders, pink flamingos, gnomes (one of our favorites), "Dot" (the plywood woman bending over), the Madonna in a bathtub, Christmas lights, dioramas, signage ("Smith Residence," for example), bird feeders, birdhouses, birdbaths, and on and on and on.

Questions to Ask About Softscaping Elements

The softscape, or planting portion of the landscape, is a dynamic element that requires a great deal of knowledge for the best design and results. Unfortunately, landscapers who start out without the benefit of a degree in landscape horticulture or who are inexperienced in growing plants will be lacking in this important information. Ignorance of a plant's growth habits can — and usually does — come back to haunt you in later years.

Often, what you need to know about a plant has to do with the growing conditions for your area, information you can get from local plant experts who have already made — and learned from — the mistakes you might otherwise be about to make yourself. Many times, plant information you can look up in a book is based on that author's experience with the plant in his or her locale. Although the information is generally true, be aware that not all of it may apply to your site. If you need to know if a plant will thrive in your location or conditions, we recommend that you get the insight of a plant professional working in your area.

Trees and Shrubs

Some general categories of concerns apply to trees and shrubs. You can deal with these concerns by asking the right questions when you purchase these plants or when a landscape designer is telling you what he or she plans to plant in your yard. Most of these issues involve the plants' growth habits. By understanding potential problems and asking about them, you can help inexperienced landscape contractors realize how their plant recommendations will affect you. This can also help keep you from making some mistakes when you are planning your own yard's design.

The height the plant will grow. Too many times, we think of plants as objects that will never change. That is definitely not the case. How many times have you seen a house with shrubs that appear to be eating the house alive? Huge old evergreens block the windows and sometimes even the door. What about planting trees under power lines? Make planting decisions by thinking of the consequences of growth, or you will set yourself up for potential problems and possible hazards.

The width of a tree canopy or a mature shrub. Some plants want to grow wide. If you plant a spreading tree with weak branches too close to a swimming pool, you will create a lot of extra cleanup and maybe a lawsuit or

When you're planting a tree, consider its proximity to power lines when full grown.

Planting a tree too close to a swimming pool may result in leaves dropping into the pool when the tree matures.

Asking the Right Questions of Contractors　137

two. Or let's say you plant two shrubs a foot and a half on either side of a four-foot walk. If that type of shrub wants to grow to six feet across, you are going to need to do a lot of pruning to keep it under control. Even if you don't mind pruning, you are likely to destroy the character of the plant that attracted you in the first place.

The shape of a tree or shrub. Plants want to grow a certain way. In our ignorance, however, we sometimes try to make a plant grow the way we want it to. A good example of this plant abuse is with yews. Different varieties of yews come in different growth forms. If you want a round ball form, you should grow a Brownii. If you want a columnar upright that doesn't get too tall, your choice would be a Hicksii. But, if you want a very short columnar upright yew, you would consider a Robusta. A low-spreading yew might be a Wardii variety. Too many times you will see someone trying to make a spreading form of yew become an upright box. The extra work and frustration of trying — and failing — to achieve your desired effect would have been avoided if the right question had been asked when the shrub was purchased. (See chapter 8 for more information.)

Branching habits and structure. The branching habits and structure of trees and shrubs can give you clues about their future. Some trees are prone to what are called "weak crotches." As the tree matures and greater weight is put on the branches by the growth of wood and leaf mass, there is an increasingly greater chance that the branch will separate from the tree and damage a house or a car, or injure a person.

Invasive roots near septic systems. Some plants love water and their roots will seek it out. If you use these plants near a septic system you will be subjecting your pipes and septic tank to invasion and costly maintenance.

Messy fruit droppings. Certain fruiting trees and shrubs will produce such messy or obnoxious fruit that it can decrease the value of your property. A good example is a mulberry tree. Birds eat the mulberry fruits and go to your or the neighbor's clothesline and defecate on the clean clothes. The stains are not easily removed. You also may have to pay for new clothes or at least a hefty dry-cleaning bill.

Susceptibility of a tree or shrub to insects and disease. Some trees and shrubs are far more likely to be attacked by debilitating pests. If the attributes of a plant outweigh its negative traits, go ahead and plant it — but at least you will have made an intelligent decision

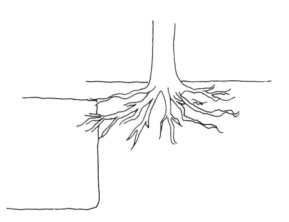

Avoid planting a water-seeking tree too close to a septic tank. The roots may crack the tank.

If the tree you're planting produces fruit, be sure the droppings are not going to damage your property or your neighbor's.

and know the problems you could face. Forewarned is forearmed.

The density of the branching pattern. If you are trying to get maximum sunlight into your home in the winter, be careful about the relative density of the normal branching pattern on a tree. If the tree reduces solar gain, you may have to spend some dollars in the not-too-distant future to prune and thin the crown of the tree.

Be careful of crossing or touching branches or tree trunks. Remember that woody plants grow out more than they grow up. The new growth will grow around whatever is in its way, even adjacent branches or tree trunks. It is not unusual for a tree to grow into itself and create a weak union that could eventually fail.

Prune at the proper time of the year. Be sure that you understand the best time to prune the trees or shrubs you have planted. When you prune largely depends on the reason for pruning, but certain rules will apply to your region and the nature of the plant you are pruning.

Cold hardiness. If you are buying trees and shrubs out of a catalog, it is hard to say if they will grow in your region. They might, but only if planted in the middle of a south-facing slope, for example. Be sure to check with local nursery or landscape professionals. You could also look for these plants growing well in your neighborhood.

Be sure to ask these questions about trees and shrubs:

1. As this tree matures, what sort of changes should I look for? Typical answers would include increased root competition, increased shade, trunk expansion, stem growth form, crown growth form, more leaves to rake.

2. Will this tree be an effective screening plant? When some trees mature, they lose their lower limbs and will not do an effective job at screening. A good example found in the northeastern United States is the white pine. It is not very tolerant of shade, and as it matures it will shade out its lower limbs. These die and become unsightly and cease to be effective at blocking views. When you are using deciduous trees or shrubs for screening, be sure to consider the density of the branching on the plant so that there is enough mass left to provide good coverage during dormancy periods.

3. What sort of cultural requirements does this tree demand? Remember that trees will perform best when given their optimum growing conditions. This means that if your tree or shrub needs a sunny slope in order to thrive, you shouldn't try to force the plant to grow in a low-lying wet area simply because you'd like it there. Meet the needs of the plant, or it — and you — will regret it. Put the right plant in the right place and it will reward you with increased value and beauty.

4. What sorts of insects and diseases can I expect to infest this tree? What are their activity cycles? What treatments, and when, will take care of them? Different types of trees are subject to their own particular pests; cycles of activity are largely dictated by the locale and time of year. For instance, in coastal states, the peak destruction period for a certain insect may vary by as much as two weeks from inland to ocean. It is always best to check with landscape or nursery professionals, your local Cooperative Extension Service, or the local university's horticulture department. Your city or town arborists may also be of help, since they should be aware of problems before you notice them.

5. Is this tree prone to weak crotches or other structural problems? It is important to be aware of a tree's potential problems, which can be alleviated by corrective pruning and regular maintenance. Be sure to have the tree properly pruned before it is planted or before it leaves the nursery.

6. Are there compatibility problems with other trees? Can you recommend plants that would work well with this tree? Some trees, such as black walnut, produce a toxic substance in their root system that discourages certain other plant life. However, the most common problem that occurs is not taking into consideration the fact that a tree's crown (the leaf mass) increases in size and will compete with surrounding trees as well as change the light conditions for the plants beneath it.

7. What sort of regular maintenance will this tree require? A regular maintenance program should include watering during drought, if the plant needs it. Regular applications of fertilizer are often recommended, but excessive fertilization can lead to detrimental levels of salt accumulation. Fertilize only if needed and not as part of a regular routine. If you live in an area subject to snow cover, mouse guards are good insurance against girdling of newly planted trees. Mice will tunnel under the snow to feast on the inner bark of trees, working their way around the trunk. A mouse guard, made of hardware cloth, plastic, wire screen, or treated paper, will protect the tree. Be sure, however, to remove mouse guards in the spring, so that the tree doesn't grow around them.

8. When I plant this tree, should I prune it? When should I prune it? Generally, prune out only dead, crossing, or broken branches when you plant a tree. If portions of the tree die back after transplanting or initial planting, prune those branches back then.

9. Should I be concerned about cold hardiness? You should not try to grow a plant beyond its hardiness zone. Your local nursery professional or horticulturist can advise you. A single house can have dramatically different "microclimates" around it, so that plants of varying degrees of hardiness will grow. If you are going to experiment with plants that are marginally hardy, it is best to use smaller, less expensive plants. These plants are more likely to assimilate to your local climate.

10. Based on my specific soil type, what sort of planting procedure do you recommend? Always conduct a soil test before planting. This will help you to determine the proper steps for healthy, robust, and valuable specimen plants in your landscape.

11. Do you deliver? If you have to take the plant home on your own, be sure to cover the foliage with a tarp or other cloth so that you do not dry out the plant. Lay the tree down if possible so the foliage won't burn or tear. Wet the rootball or other container, but only the top inch or so. If there is too much water the ball will become excessively heavy and difficult to move. It also may be more prone to breaking apart. Once you are home, take care in unloading and get help if it is too heavy. Be sure to water the plant thoroughly and put it in the ground as soon as possible. If the landscaper does deliver, be sure these procedures are followed.

12. How much water should I give this plant at each watering and how often?

Herbaceous Plantings

Herbaceous plants are different from the woody plants that make up the "skeleton" of the landscape. They are usually seasonal in nature and are far more portable than maturing trees and shrubs. Typical herbaceous plants you will find in the garden are perennials, annuals, biennials, bulbs, corms, tubers, and vines (although vines can often be woody plants). Although they share some of the same requirements as the woodies, these plants are also subject to their own specific needs.

Invasive (rapidly spreading) plants. It is important to know how invasive a plant is likely to be given the right growing conditions. A single plant has been known to consume the entire landscape by covering or crowding out other plants, as well as covering all of the hardscape elements. For example, even though kudzu, ajuga, bishop's weed, and bittersweet can be used effectively in certain landscapes, they can also be invasive.

Maintenance (deadheading, dividing, fertilizing, etc.). How much maintenance is likely to be involved with the flowering plants you might choose? If you regard maintenance as therapeutic, don't be concerned. If, however, you think of maintenance as something to be avoided, carefully consider the choices before you. For instance, if you like irises but are not interested in spending a lot of time on care, you would likely choose Siberian iris, because it doesn't need as much work.

Length and sequence of bloom cycle. If you are planning your garden's flowering patterns, you need to know if flowers will compete with each other. How long will the flowers be blooming? Will they repeat? Can they be made to repeat?

Color and texture compatibility. Are the colors and leaf textures of the plants compatible with each other? Do they work well with the structures on the property? What happens as they mature?

Height of plant. How tall will the plant be and, more important, how tall will the flowers be if they are on a stalk above the plant? Are there other plant choices of the same species but different varieties with the height you want?

Ask these questions about herbaceous plants:

1. What sorts of changes can I expect to see in this plant as it matures? How big will it get? Will it retain its current form? Is it invasive?

2. How often will it need to be divided?

3. What are its cultural needs (drainage, fertility, etc.)?

4. How hardy is this plant?

5. How much sun does this plant require?

6. What sorts of pests and diseases can I expect and what are their activity cycles? What can be done to prevent and/or cure the problems they can cause?

7. Are these good cutting flowers?

8. Do they require deadheading?

9. What is the earliest that I can plant these annuals?

10. What kind of fall maintenance is important?

11. What kind of spring maintenance is important?

12. Is this plant field-grown or is it bareroot-potted? You generally pay more for a field-grown flower, since it is larger and will probably bloom the first year.

13. What sorts of plants would look good together or will be good companions to the ones I already have? A contrast in texture, color, or form can create an interesting landscape. In addition, some plants' cultural relationships are mutually beneficial. For example, roses like to be planted near garlic. Chives help repel scab in apple trees.

Lawn Concerns

Although the lawn-care industry would like it to be so, not every country in the world has the intense love affair with the grass lawn that America does. It is an out-and-out passion. It certainly must have something going for it to make it worthwhile to contend with the incredible amount of maintenance required to keep a relatively neat appearance. If you are one of these passionate people, you should be aware of how you can make sure the grass is always greener on your side of the fence.

pH!pH!pH!. An improper pH practically assures you of nongrowth and weeds! Your lawn needs to be growing at the proper pH or it will be unable to absorb the nutrients necessary for its health. You do not need to know all the complexities of soil chemistry, but you should at least understand how pH can affect the ability of your lawn to thrive and fend off diseases and other stressful situations. (See the glossary for more information.)

Shade. Where light is insufficient to grow grass, you should consider using an alternative ground cover, planting a shade-tolerant grass variety, or thinning or removing any light-blocking trees.

The right seed for the type of slopes you have. Some grass varieties do better on slopes than others do. You may need to consider blending several types of seed together at planting time so that different ones will dominate according to the conditions they thrive in.

The right seed for the amount of foot traffic the area will get. Some grasses will tolerate a large amount of foot traffic and others just about disappear if trampled on.

Be familiar with the control techniques appropriate to your region and type of lawn. Mowing, watering, fertilizing, liming, and insect/disease control will all vary according to where you live, the cultural requirements of the grass type, and how you intend to use your lawn.

Don't use too much seed. As the seed germinates there can be severe competition for soil moisture, nutrients, sun, and space. The resulting condition is similar to having a weed-infested lawn. If most of the seed germinates, the height of the new growth will collapse and suffocate itself. This varies with different types of grass seed, so it is always best to follow the dispersal rate or seeding pattern indicated by the seed producer.

Keep your lawn-mower blades balanced and sharp. When lawn-mower blades are dull, they have a tendency to shatter or break the ends of the blades of grass, pulling on the grass rather than cutting it. This can be devastating to a new lawn, because the new grass has not established a strong root system and the mower is likely to pull it out by the roots. An unbalanced blade will scalp one side of the mowing path and can kill off "strips" of lawn. Imagine the frustration and disappointment you will feel after all the time and trouble you spent nurturing your brand-new lawn, if you then destroy some or all of the new grass — all because you didn't attend to a minor maintenance issue.

Keep the lawn properly aerated. Continued walking and playing on a lawn area can compact the soil and cause stress on the lawn as well as the surrounding trees and shrubs. Compaction breaks down the air spaces in the soil essential for good plant growth. The air spaces provide places for oxygen exchange and for percolation of water through the soil.

Keep the lawn properly dethatched. Continued mowings, annual die-back, and the over-fertilization of lawns contribute to the problem of thatch. Excessive fertilizing also tends to decrease the pH of the soil, which then leads to a decrease in microbial activity, resulting in more thatch. The grass becomes yellow and unhealthy looking. Thatch buildup reduces air, nutrients, and moisture in the soil.

Dogs. Dogs are not good companions for your lawn. They like to dig, run wild, and urinate. Spots caused by urine are often mistaken for diseases such as fairy rings, dollar spot, and brown patch. Watering helps to dilute the ammonia found in urine, but it is best to keep dogs off new lawns.

Buried debris. Buried debris can be any number of things. The most likely objects to cause problems are stumps, building refuse, and stones. When they are close to the surface, they can cause a moisture deficit that makes the grass die back. Stumps and logs can cause soil slumping as they decay. They can also be responsible for fungal growth, such as mushrooms and fairy rings. In areas where frost is an annual event, stones buried in the lawn can be lifted by the ice in the ground to the surface. You may have traveled on a road for years and then suddenly notice a new bump in the surface. This bump later turned out to be a stone. The same thing can happen in your yard.

Moss. It takes a number of conditions to grow moss: poor air circulation, low fertility, high compaction, and high air-moisture content. In most cases, shade and acidity are also contributing factors. Lime does not always correct mossy conditions, but is used to raise the soil pH. There are two options for dealing with moss. The first is to learn to love it and the second is to break the chain of conditions that make it grow.

Algae. Algal growth relies on high fertility and weak, thin turf. It is most often found in low-lying, compacted, shaded, and wet areas. An indication of past algal growth is a thick black crust that is cracked and peeling like the dried surface of chocolate pudding.

Drought or desiccation. Certain types of grasses are more susceptible to drought than others. For instance, deep-rooted species such as the tall turf-type fescues are far more resistant to dry conditions than Kentucky bluegrasses. Each lawn's situation is unique and you need to ask the opinion of local nursery or landscape professionals.

Scald. In low areas where water from rain or irrigation is retained, and extreme heat occurs, the lawn can be killed through a scalding process. Be sure to have sufficient drainage in any low-lying areas, especially if you are in a hot climate with clay soils.

Heaving. This is a problem in northern climates and occurs in newly seeded lawns. Frost heaving pushes the grass above the finished grade and exposes the crowns of the plants to wind, which will desiccate and kill the grasses.

Ice injury. When ice accumulates in low-lying areas of the yard, you can injure your turf by reduced transpiration. This is caused by thick layers of ice that stay in one place for a long time. Again, be sure to have adequate drainage in your new lawn.

Salt injury. Lawn areas next to walks, roads, and driveways are targets for salt damage. You can use a salt-tolerant grass or you can treat the area each year by flushing the salt out with water or by applying calcium sulfate (gypsum).

Late spring frost. When the new spring grass growth is killed by a late frost, the food reserves stored in that portion of the plant are lost. If this process is repeated several times during the course of the year, the plant itself can die.

Winter desiccation. This is sometimes known as "windburn" and occurs on exposed slopes subject to fast runoff and low water levels. Since these areas are open to winter winds, the crowns of the grass plants can be killed.

Insects. If there is a problem in your area with Japanese beetles or rose chafers, try to get all of your neighbors on a lawn-care program to control the grubs.

Chemicals in the groundwater. Consider an organic approach to lawn care — the misuse of chemicals by homeowners is a serious threat to our groundwater.

Timing of seeding. For best results, plant a new lawn in the early fall. Dormant seeding, or planting grass seed in the late fall or early winter when the ground temperature is too low to cause germination, can also be effective. Spring seeding works well, too; however, a greater number of weeds may grow. Do not plant in the summer unless you have a regular and adequate supply of water.

Water. Lawns love water. If you live in an area where water conservation is a priority, be sure to use amended soils with effective water retention. This can be a real value, saving significant dollars in the long run. This is especially true where water costs are high or where there are watering restrictions.

Ask these questions when buying grass seed or having a lawn done professionally:

1. Is this seed an annual or perennial? If it is blended, be sure that most of the seed is perennial.

2. What is the rate of application? Seed mixes with great deal of chaff require you to apply large quantities for good coverage. This seed appears to be cheap but will cost you more in the long run, since the mix contains a high percentage of inert matter (indicated on the bag or box).

3. What is the germination rate? Be careful of seed mixes with germination rates lower than sixty percent, because more seed will be required.

4. How quickly will it germinate? The rate of germination varies depending on the time of year, and different types of seed have various germination rates. If you have a blended mixture of grasses that will germinate at different times, you need to extend your initial watering program to accommodate all the grasses that will be sprouting. The first flush of grass you see may be from only one of the grasses in your mixture.

5. How tolerant is this grass mixture to shade? to drought? to disease? to foot traffic? to high moisture areas? to slopes?

6. What is the proper mowing height and frequency for this type of grass and in this region? In areas that are arid or are subject to dry spells, you should mow your lawn at the highest setting on your mower, usually two and a half inches. This helps to protect the crowns of the grass from the heat of the sun and from drying out.

7. How tall should the grass be when I mow for the first and all subsequent mowings? When you mow for the first time you should never take off more than one-third of the total height. A quick and dirty rule: "As

the new grass begins to bend, it's time to mow." This is usually a height of about three and a half inches.

8. What is the best time of the year to fertilize and lime? Generally speaking, liming should be done in the fall or early spring. The lime takes sixty to ninety days from application to break down in the soil. The best time to fertilize is in the late fall. At this time the roots are expanding and will take in nitrogen and store it for use next spring. Another good time to fertilize is when water is abundant in your region. As always, be sure to check with landscape professionals in your area before you apply any fertilizers or lime. They can advise about the quantity and type appropriate for your conditions. The importance of having a periodic soil test to determine levels of pH and nutrients in the soil can't be overstated. Habitual liming and fertilizing not only can be costly, but also can be detrimental to your lawn. Be sure to have your soil tested!

9. If using hay for a mulch after seeding, when should I remove any excess? When grass begins to germinate it will usually push through the hay mulch. However, if you have left a sizable clump of hay, you should remove it when you see it starting to rise off the ground. This means that the grass has germinated and is pushing it. The grass will quickly die if not allowed to receive sunlight. The rest of the loose hay in your lawn can remain there as it decomposes; it will add nutrients to the soil. The lawn-mower will help in breaking down the hay by chopping it up.

10. How often should I water and how much should be used? A number of variables help determine watering rate. Temperature, humidity, soil type, wind, type of grass, and length of daylight can influence the amount of water needed. Generally speaking, the ground should be kept moist, but not saturated. A good trick for determining how much water is being applied is to place an empty glass jar under the sprinkler. Time how long it takes for the jar to fill with the desired amount of water (usually fifteen to twenty minutes per inch). This tells you how long to water. Remember, a soil of average porosity takes an inch above the ground to soak six inches below. Sometimes a break in watering is necessary to allow water to be absorbed before continuing.

11. Will you be using screened loam? Screened loam will make the spreading process much easier and is worth the extra money. Screening eliminates rocks and other large debris that otherwise would be working their way to the surface constantly.

12. Will the loam be spread at least four inches deep? This is very important, because a lawn without an adequate loam base will not have a good root system and is more susceptible to drought and disease.

13. Has a pH test been done? Has a fertility or nutrient test been done? The answer should be yes.

14. Which is the better option, sodding or seeding? If you have sod installed, be sure to maintain properly. This can't be overstated. Do not take this advice lightly. Improperly maintained sod will deteriorate rapidly. We have seen commercial sod applications that looked horrible after only one year of neglect. Sod is typically composed of bluegrass varieties that, as a rule, have an extremely high need for nitrogen and are susceptible to a number of diseases.

15. Has this seed been endophytically treated? In most cases this is a positive thing. Endophytically treated grass seed is generally more resistant to insect and disease problems and appears healthier. (See the glossary for more information.) Problems arise if you or your neighbors have horses grazing on the lawn. This treatment will give them the "shakes."

Appendices

Appendix I

How Valuable Is Your Home Landscape?
A Proposed Aesthetic Evaluation Model

QUANTIFYING PROPERTY VALUE ADDED OR lost as a result of aesthetics requires a set of objective criteria for judging. The real estate marketplace needs a tool that could be used for assessing the contribution "good landscaping" makes to a property. The obvious source for these criteria is generally accepted principles of design. By looking closely at practical applications of these design principles, we have set up a scale with ranges for assessing how well a particular landscape fulfills each principle.

One landscape architect who has begun to identify practical ways to assess design principles is Joseph Hudak, based in Westwood, Massachusetts. His basic analysis begins with the identification of two principles: function and order. According to Hudak, good design looks at how well the function of the landscape is achieved and if there is an overall order to the composition. Function relates directly to the needs of the site and the user. Order, however, Hudak says, is a bit more complex. It is comprised of

a number of components, including unity, repetition, sequence, balance, proportion, rhythm, dominance, and contrast. The principles Hudak has identified can be applied to pricing and evaluating real estate. First, some of the terms listed above need translating to work in the context of real estate.

We have shaped Hudak's analysis into a practical evaluative tool for determining how well the design principles have been applied to increase the value of a particular piece of property. This model is experimental and needs to undergo extensive testing to establish its validity. If any real estate or insurance professionals decide to team up with landscape design professionals in their area to initiate a further study into the proof and applications of this model, we would greatly appreciate any feedback you could provide as a result of those studies.

This model includes a series of scales to help you assess how well a landscape meets a variety of design elements. Following is a greatly simplified homeowner's version of this model that you can use to assess the value of your landscape. Tally the results, then come back and tally them again after you've made improvements.

Unity can be translated to mean "curb appeal," since that is the first view of the property that a potential buyer is likely to have. Unity may also describe other perspectives gained on the property, such as the view from a picture window or a deck. In general real estate terms, unity refers to a client's first impression — does the property come across as having a harmonious, well-integrated appearance?

Definition of Design Elements

First Impression. This "curb appeal" is of a high priority in considering the value of aesthetics. It is this impression that sets a tone and a memory of the home. It is an amalgamation of all of the various aesthetic factors.

Sustainability. When we speak of sustainability, maintenance is the major concern. You might ask, "Does the landscape require a great deal of time, effort, and money to keep it attractive? Is mowing difficult? Are there large areas of mulched bed with a low planting density?"

Function. When you think of function in the landscape, you are considering how different elements are to be used. Good questions might be, "Do the functional aspects of the landscape work well? Are the walkways too narrow? Is the tread on the steps too high or shallow? Are benches at a comfortable height? Are views blocked where they should be enhanced?" The functions of any landscape are unique and need to be measured on a case-by-case basis.

Visual Flow. Visual Flow is how the eye moves through the landscape. When done well, the eye easily focuses to the areas that are the most attractive. It usually predicates the physical flow through the landscape and makes evident the path one needs to follow.

Context to Architecture. In creating proper context to a building's architecture, the planting and hardscape design should complement the structures they surround. "Is there a continuity between the buildings, including any outbuildings and the landscape? If the architecture is of a historical time period, does the landscape reflect that same era?" are questions you might ask when considering the landscape and its relationship to your site's buildings.

Context to Site. This type of context is making the design of the landscape consistent with other landscaping in the area. The landscape elements in the designed space may reflect a unique aspect of the site or region.

Balance. Balance in a landscape is achieved when the yard has a feeling of appropriate distribution of elements. In a formal landscape design, one should be able to draw a line down the middle of the space and one side would be like a reflection of the other. If the design is based on a more natural model, the balance should be informal. Look for the use of triangle arrangements of various objects (stone, plant, hardscape elements).

Depth. Depth relates to how deep the landscape or space feels. This is achieved by creating a foreground, midground, and background within the space. Depth can also be created by repeating common elements in the landscape at reduced scales.

Color. Although color can be considered as simply one of the contrasting elements, it needs to be separate for the purposes of aesthetic evaluation. It is a major influencing factor in regard to emotional response to a built landscape and needs to be looked at separately. Complementary colors and continual bloom that work in conjunction with surrounding colors (e.g., house paint) are things to look for.

Framing. A fine picture becomes even better when it is properly matted and framed. The same applies to a landscape. This type of framing is accomplished by creating horizontal and vertical elements to enclose a view. You also need to consider where you will be viewing the landscape from: the road, the walk, the front door, a picture window, a deck, a patio, etc.

Contrast. Contrast is the comparison of opposites. Using elements together that are in contrast to each other can enhance the view of the landscape. Contrast can be a way of creating interest and facilitating visual flow in the built landscape. A pitfall can be if you create contrast just for the sake of creating contrast. When done well, contrast feels natural and not contrived.

Related Elements to Understand

The following essential components of good design (as related by Hudak) are translated into the terms used in the aesthetic evaluation model:

Unity. Unity is closely related to curb appeal, since this is the factor that most influences a potential buyer's first impression of the property. In general real estate terms, unity refers to a client's first impression — i.e., does the property come across as having a unified, well-integrated appearance? Unity can also be applied to perspectives gained from other areas of the property, such as the view from a picture window or a deck.

Repetition. Repetition is the reusing of certain elements in the landscape and can be used in a variety of ways. Used properly, it can enhance the feeling of depth. It can also facilitate the visual flow and it can emphasize formal and informal balance.

Sequence. Sequence is the order in which elements are placed. When objects are out of sequence it tends to disrupt the visual flow.

Balance. Balance in the landscape is when elements are placed in a way that is stable and comfortable to view.

Proportion. Proportion refers to the comparative relationships of elements in the landscape as to size. When elements of any design have a correct relationship to each other in terms of size, they are in scale and can create a feeling of depth in the landscsape. When the elements are out of proportion, scale is destroyed.

Rhythm. Rhythm is like a tempo or beat but in the landscape, rather than aural it is visual in nature. The proper use of rhythm in the design of a landscape creates good visual flow.

Dominance. Dominance is where an element or a group of objects commands attention. It is related to framing and visual flow in the design of a space. By using framing well, you can have a scene achieve a great deal of dominance or importance. Visual flow can enhance or facilitate the viewing of a dominant object.

Contrast. Contrast is the comparison of opposites. Using contrasting elements together can enhance the view of the landscape. It can be related to and used to create visual flow. Examples of elements that are used in contrast are textures, lines, forms, shapes, and color.

In addition to the above aesthetic and functional considerations there are also the issues of sustainability and context (to architecture and site) that affect the value of the landscape on a property.

LANDSCAPE ELEMENTS MOST LIKELY TO INFLUENCE REAL ESTATE VALUE

In order of their relative importance, beginning with the most important (which will always be debatable), following are the elements that have an impact on real estate value:

> First Impression
> Sustainability
> Function
> Visual Flow
> Context to Architecture
> Context to Site
> Balance
> Depth
> Color
> Framing
> Contrast

How to Use This Tool

The following tally sheet allows you to "grade" how well your own landscape measures up to the above criteria. Although it is subjective, when you are done, you will have a good idea of what is missing or what needs to be enhanced. Evaluate each of the criteria (based on your own feelings and the definition of the term) on a scale of 1 to 10. By using the opinions of others (friends or family), you can create a good average. Take that number times the ranking (provided) and you have your score for that criterion. Add all of the scores together to determine where your landscape falls on the grading scale.

HOW DOES YOUR LANDSCAPE RATE?

Formula: Rating x Weighting Factor = Score

Element	Your Rating (from 0 to 10)		Weighting Factor		Score
First Impression	____	x	11	=	____
Sustainability	____	x	10	=	____
Function	____	x	9	=	____
Visual Flow	____	x	8	=	____
Context to Architecture	____	x	7	=	____
Context to Site	____	x	6	=	____
Balance	____	x	5	=	____
Depth	____	x	4	=	____
Color	____	x	3	=	____
Framing	____	x	2	=	____
Contrast	____	x	1	=	____
				TOTAL	____

Score	
0 to 260	Poor
261 to 440	Fair
441 to 540	Good
541 to 620	Very Good
621 to 660	Excellent

Landscape Assessment Sample Rating

Formula: Rating x Weighting Factor = Score

Element	Sample Rating (from 0 to 10)	Weighting Factor	Score
First Impression	9	11	99
Sustainability	9	10	90
Function	7	9	63
Visual Flow	9	8	72
Context to Architecture	7	7	49
Context to Site	8	6	48
Balance	9	5	45
Depth	8	4	32
Color	9	3	27
Framing	8	2	16
Contrast	8	1	8
		TOTAL	549

Appendix 2

USDA Hardiness Zone Map

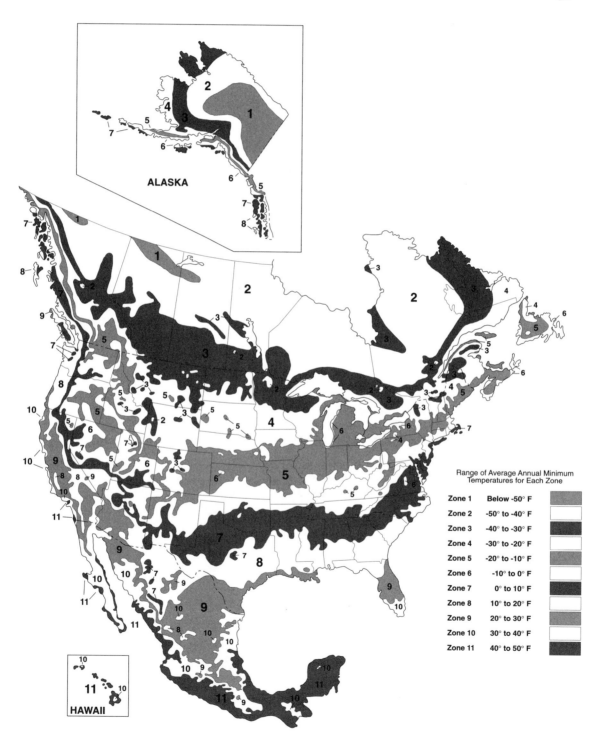

ALASKA

Range of Average Annual Minimum Temperatures for Each Zone

Zone 1	Below -50° F
Zone 2	-50° to -40° F
Zone 3	-40° to -30° F
Zone 4	-30° to -20° F
Zone 5	-20° to -10° F
Zone 6	-10° to 0° F
Zone 7	0° to 10° F
Zone 8	10° to 20° F
Zone 9	20° to 30° F
Zone 10	30° to 40° F
Zone 11	40° to 50° F

HAWAII

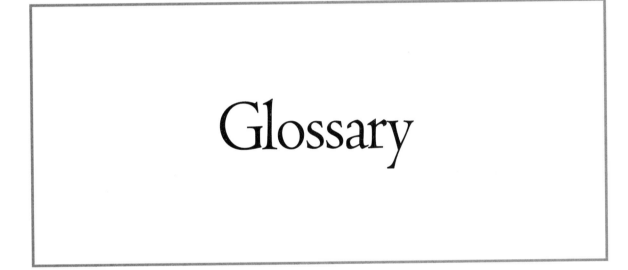

Glossary

12-Volt Lighting. Low-voltage lighting is frequently used in the landscape. A transformer is used to reduce the voltage from 120 volts to 12 volts. This is advantageous mainly for the safety of the homeowner and because lower voltage will translate into lower power bills.

Aerial Method. The practice of fertilization by means of spray and absorption. An example of this is Miracle-Gro or Rapid-Gro liquid fertilizer applied with a sprayer.

Alpine Plants. Plants that grow in the mountains. These plants are noted for their ability to thrive in conditions of low fertility and very fast drainage.

Annual. A plant that lives for one season. It starts the season as a seed; it then sprouts, grows foliage, and produces flowers and seed in one growing season. Annuals are popular because they produce consistent blooms through the summer for northern gardens.

Arboriculture. A study or discipline that deals with the cultivation and understanding of trees.

Arborist. A person who is knowledgeable in the cultivation and care of trees.

B&B. Refers to the method of root preparation for transplanting. The acronym refers to *balled and burlapped*. It is usually used at nurseries for larger plants.

Bareroot. Plants that are shipped and planted without the benefit (or weight and cost) of soil.

Basal Area. The area occupied by a cross-section of a tree trunk.

Batter. A backward and upward slope to the face of a wall. Used to create structural stability.

Biennial. A plant that lives for two years. This plant germinates and produces foliage in the first season. It then goes on to produce foliage, blooms, and seed in the second season.

Bluestone. A quarried sedimentary stone usually one to two inches thick sawed into squares, rectangles, and irregular shapes for paving purposes. Ranges in color from blue to green to gray.

Bog Plants. Plants that are specific to floating sphagnum wetlands.

Bracing. The stabilization of a splitting tree by the use of rods and oval plates, usually pulled together with nuts.

Broadcast Method. The practice of fertilization that spreads fertilizer evenly over a wide area.

Bulbs. Modified underground stems surrounded by scalelike modified leaves. Examples are daffodils, tulips, and crocuses.

Cabling. The stabilization of two or more tree branches or stems that are in danger of splitting because of weak crotches.

Cell Pacs. Plant packaging method using peat moss or plastic to contain a seedling. Usually six or more seedlings per pac.

Cistern. A man-made tank or dammed area used for holding water. It can also be a naturally occurring hollow that holds water. It often is covered or capped.

Concrete Sand. A type or grade of aggregate used to make concrete. It has sharp, flat edges and compacts well, thus making it a good material for flat dry masonry such as patios.

Container-Grown. Plants that are planted and grown in canisters usually made of plastic, or occasionally metal.

Contractor. A person or company that performs the supply, installation, and construction of the landscape.

Corm. An underground stem similar to a bulb, but with no scales. An example is the gladiolus.

Cribbing. In timber construction, the practice of using pieces of timber placed perpendicular to the face of the wall and connecting them to form a box. The soils behind the wall are then used to fill the area and are compacted. The box or crib is placed below the surface for greater stability. This system of construction helps to keep the wall standing and plumb.

Crotch. The area where two or more branches converge.

Crown. The area of a plant between the root system and the foliage.

Crushed Stone. Usually produced in quarries, it is the end product of blasting and sending stone through a crusher. It does not have small aggregate, sand, or silt mixed in the end product; it should be just stone.

Deadhead. The process of removing a spent flower blossom.

Deadman. In timber-retaining wall construction, a piece of timber going back into the banking. It is connected to the main wall and is perpendicular to the face of the wall. This construction method is used to keep the wall plumb.

Deciduous. A term used to describe plants that lose their leaves. Some examples are oak, viburnum, euonymus, and maple.

Deep-Root Fertilization. The practice of fertilization by pressurized application of water and fertilizer into the ground.

Desiccation. The process of drying out.

Drill Method. The practice of fertilization by pouring granular fertilizer into a hole in the ground usually produced with a crowbar.

Drip Edge. An area under the eaves of a building that usually consists of crushed stone that rainwater or snowmelt runs into.

Drip Line. The imaginary line at the edge of the leaf mass of trees or shrubs. In a light rain the area between the drip line and the stem or trunk will be dry.

Dry Laid. A method of masonry that does not use mortar or concrete.

Duck-Bill Anchor. An anchoring device resembling a duck's bill made of metal and wire that is driven into the ground with the aid of a metal rod. When the wire is pulled tight, the "duck bill" flips in the soil and becomes locked in place, thus providing the basis for guying a tree in place.

Edging. A manufactured product of metal or plastic shaped like an L or T. It is usually anchored with spikes and is used on the outermost course of bricks to contain the work.

Emergent. In the context of water plants, *emergent* refers to plants with their roots submerged and the leaf portions of the plants erect and standing above the water.

Endophytes. Fungal organisms that live symbiotically within grass plants. They reproduce when the grass cells divide. They impart a bitter taste to grasses, which discourages insects that feed on grass. Endophyte infection should be at least 70 percent or higher to be effective.

Endophytic. A plant living within another, but not in a parasitic state.

Evergreen. Plants that retain their leaves or needles and are green throughout the year, such as white pine and rhododendron.

Fieldstone. The stone used in the walls around cultivated land, usually associated with traditional American farmland.

Flagstone. A very hard slate ranging in color from red to green to gray to blue; usually only an inch or so in thickness. It is used in patios, walks, etc.

Freestanding Wall. A wall made of stone with three finished sides — the cap as well as the two sides.

French Parterre. A walled garden with flower beds arranged in formal balance. Walks run parallel to the walls, and in most cases a fountain is in the center of the garden.

"G" Scale Railroad. A fairly large scale of railroad used by railroad enthusiasts who like to have their railroads surrounded by gardens.

Gazebo. An outdoor structure often shaped as a polygon that is freestanding with a roof and an entry.

Geotextile. A manufactured woven or spun fabric that allows moisture and gases to pass but will impede the development of weeds and helps to separate aggregates of different densities.

Girdling Root. A root that grows around the tree that it comes from. It can eventually kill the tree.

Gravel. Stone mixed with small aggregate and sand particles. A typical use would be for an unpaved driveway.

Ground Cover. A plant used alone for covering a large area. Examples are grass, periwinkle, pachysandra, and juniper.

Groundwater. A term used to describe the water found in the earth.

Hardiness Zone. A series of zones determined by the average lowest temperatures found in a particular geographic region.

Hardscape. The nonliving component of the landscape. Examples are patios and walls.

Herbaceous. A nonwoody tissue plant such as grass.

Hydroseeding. A seeding application where seed is combined and agitated with fertilizer, mulch, sticking agent, and water, producing a slurry that is sprayed out under pressure onto a prepared soil surface.

Injection Method. The practice of fertilization by putting fertilizer directly into the cambium (the growth tissue) of the plant. This is often done by means of a capsule.

Landscape Architect. A person who has a degree in landscape architecture and has fulfilled an apprenticeship of usually two years.

Landscape Designer. A person who is knowledgeable in design and horticulture.

Leader. A dominant stem on a tree or shrub.

Liverwort. A primitive non-flowering plant related to ferns and mosses noted for its horizontal growth.

Loam. Soil that consists of defined levels of sand, clay, silt, and organic material.

Lycopodium. A primitive, spore-producing, non-flowering plant also known as "club moss."

Microclimate. An environmental situation created by a variety of factors. Proximity to a large body of water or shelter from trees can influence the ability of plants to grow and thrive that otherwise would be outside their hardiness zone.

Moss. A primitive, spore-producing plant that generally likes moist, low-fertility, and shady conditions.

Mouse Guard. A sleeve or screen that fits around the base of a trunk or ground stem of a plant and acts as a barrier to invading rodents (not just mice).

MSDS. An acronym for Material Safety Data Sheets. These sheets are required by law to be carried by contractors covering any hazardous material they use in the course of performing their business. These sheets should be in the contractors' vehicles and they should have an understanding of their contents.

Mulch. Any substance that is used for moisture retention and/or weed inhibition.

Naturalizing. Re-establishing an apparently natural state or condition.

Nurseryperson. A person who is involved in the production and cultivation of plants for resale.

Patio. A flat, paved area used as an outdoor sitting place.

Pea Stone. A grade of stone defined by its size (usually less than ⅜ inch).

Perennial. A herbaceous plant that grows back from its dormant state year after year.

Pergola. An outdoor structure that acts as a passageway.

Percolation. The movement of water through the soil. A sandy soil is said to "perc" well. This is a slang term that was derived from *percolate*.

Permaculture. A design discipline originated in Australia by Bill Mollison that regards the plan of the landscape as zones of usage radiating outward from the residence. The higher the maintenance, the closer it is to the home. *Permaculture* is a contraction of "permanent" and "agriculture." One of its common precepts is that all plants that are used should have at least two functions.

Pesticide. Any product that is used to control insect pests. Sevin, for example, may be used to kill aphids or whiteflies. Soaps are also included in this definition if used for pest control.

pH. The relative measure of acid and/or alkaline levels in a substance. Usually it is a measuring tool for gardeners to use in monitoring a soil. The scale is from 1–14. Neutral is 7, below 7 is acid, and above 7 is alkaline.

Pipe-Puller. A mechanical system used in irrigation to pull pipes through the existing ground without trenching or digging, to lessen the impact on root systems of surrounding trees.

Porosity. The quality of being porous or permeable by water or air.

Ramada. An outdoor shelter with a thatched roof and open sides.

Retaining Wall. A wall that holds back a slope or creates a raised bed.

River Jack. A term referring to smooth stone as it might be tumbled by moving water. Frequently used as decorative stone.

Rootball. A globe of soil that contains the roots of a plant. The best rootball is really not a globe, but is rather flat on the surface.

Root Suffocation. The diminishing of the gas exchange necessary for the survival of a plant by the compaction of soil or the raising of the grade surrounding the plant.

Sailor Rows. Bricks placed vertically with the wider side toward the pavement to form a border around patios, walkways, and other paved surfaces.

Sleeve Fence. A fence commonly found in Japan. It is called "sleeve" fence because it is attached to a building much like a sleeve is attached to a shirt or coat. The construction materials and design should echo the architecture of the structure to which it is attached.

Slumping. An area of diminished elevation which can be caused by decaying stumps. It can also describe the activity of soil on a slope that is shifting downward.

Softscape. The living part of the landscape. It includes all plants.

Soldier Rows. Bricks placed vertically with the narrow side toward the pavement to form a border around patios, walkways, and other paved surfaces.

Spike. The practice of fertilization by driving a solid rod of fertilizer into the ground.

Terrace. A flat, level area within a slope.

Transpiration. The passing of moisture usually through the leaves and stems of a plant.

Tree Canopy. The foliar part of a tree.

Tuber. A swollen underground stem bearing buds from which new plants emerge, such as a potato.

Undermining. The action that takes place when moving water pulls soils out from behind or under a structure.

Wet Laid. A masonry term meaning that concrete or mortar is used in the construction process.

Xeriscape. A landscape practice that uses plants with high drought tolerance.

Well. The most common types of wells are dug, driven point, drilled, and artesian. A dug well is usually dug by hand or backhoe and uses the groundwater as its source. These wells are usually found in areas with a relatively high water table and easy digging. A driven point well consists of an uptake pipe driven into the ground and is found in areas with extremely high water tables. A drilled well goes deeper in the ground and is often used where the water table is low or the water is found in fractured stone at great depth. In an artesian well, water rises under natural pressure.

Woodland Plants. Plants found in the understory of the forest; the *understory* is the plant community under the canopy of the dominant trees.

For Further Reading

General Landscaping

Bookout, Lloyd W. *Value By Design: Landscape, Site Planning, & Amenities.* Washington, D.C.: Urban Land Institute, 1994.

Binetti, Marianne. *Shortcuts for Accenting Your Garden: Over 500 Easy and Inexpensive Tips.* Pownal, VT: Storey Publishing, 1993.

———. *Tips for Carefree Landscapes: Over 500 Sure-fire Ways to Beautify Your Yard and Garden.* Pownal, VT: Garden Way Publishing, 1990.

Dubé, Richard. *Natural Pattern Forms.* New York: Van Nostrand Reinhold, 1997.

Franklin, Stuart. *Building a Healthy Lawn: A Safe and Natural Approach.* Pownal, VT: Storey Publishing, 1988.

Hardscaping

Braren, Ken, and Roger Griffith. *HomeMade: 101 Easy-to-Make Things for Your Garden, Home, or Farm.* Pownal, VT: Storey Publishing, 1977.

Burch, Monte. *Building Small Barns, Sheds & Shelters.* Pownal, VT: Storey Publishing, 1983.

———. *64 Yard & Garden Projects You Can Build Yourself.* Pownal, VT: Storey Publishing, 1994.

Damerow, Gail. *Fences for Pasture & Garden.* Pownal, VT: Storey Publishing, 1992.

Lawrence, Mike. *Play Equipment for Kids: Great Projects You Can Build.* Pownal, VT: Storey Publishing, 1996.

———(ed.). *Step-by-Step Outdoor Stonework.* Pownal, VT: Storey Publishing, 1995.

McRaven, Charles. *Building with Stone.* Pownal, VT: Storey Publishing, 1989.

Ramuz, Mark. *Birdhouses: 20 Step-by-Step Woodworking Projects.* Pownal, VT: Storey Publishing, 1996.

Vivian, John. *Building Stone Walls.* Pownal, VT: Storey Publishing, 1979.

Whitner, Jan Kowalczewski. *Stonescaping: A Guide to Using Stone in Your Garden.* Pownal, VT: Storey Publishing, 1992.

Woodson, R. Dodge. *Watering Systems for Lawn & Garden: A Do-It-Yourself Guide.* Pownal, VT: Storey Publishing, 1996.

Softscaping/General Gardening

Editors of Garden Way Publishing. *The Big Book of Gardening Skills.* Pownal, VT: Garden Way Publishing, 1993.

Hart, Rhonda Massingham. *Bugs, Slugs & Other Thugs: Controlling Garden Pests Organically.* Pownal, VT: Storey Publishing, 1991.

————. *Dirt-Cheap Gardening: Hundreds of Ways to Save Money in Your Garden.* Pownal, VT: Storey Publishing, 1995.

Macunovich, Janet. *Easy Garden Design: 12 Simple Steps to Creating Successful Gardens and Land-scapes.* Pownal, VT: Storey Publishing, 1992.

Pleasant, Barbara. *The Gardener's Bug Book: Earth-Safe Insect Control.* Pownal, VT: Storey Publishing, 1994.

————. *The Gardener's Guide to Plant Diseases: Earth-Safe Remedies.* Pownal, VT: Storey Publishing, 1995.

————. *The Gardener's Weed Book: Earth-Safe Controls.* Pownal, VT: Storey Publishing, 1996.

Powell, Eileen. *From Seed to Bloom: How to Grow over 500 Annuals, Perennials & Herbs.* Pownal, VT: Storey Publishing, 1995.

Raymond, Dick. *Down-to-Earth Natural Lawn Care.* Pownal, VT: Storey Publishing, 1993.

————. *Garden Way's Joy of Gardening.* Pownal, VT: Storey Publishing, 1983.

Riotte, Louise. *Roses Love Garlic. Secrets of Companion Planting with Flowers.* Pownal, VT: Storey Publishing, 1983.

————. *Successful Small Food Gardens: Vegetables, Herbs, Flowers, Fruits, Nuts, Berries.* Pownal, VT: Storey Publishing, 1993.

Sears, Elayne. *Step-by-Step Gardening Techniques Illustrated.* Pownal, VT: Garden Way Publishing, 1995.

Tilgner, Linda. *Tips for the Lazy Gardener.* Pownal, VT: Storey Publishing, 1985.

Softscaping/Specialized Techniques and Plants

Art, Henry W. *A Garden of Wildflowers: 101 Native Species and How to Grow Them.* Pownal, VT: Storey Publishing, 1986.

Brooklyn Botanic Garden. *Annuals: A Gardener's Guide.* Brooklyn, NY: Brooklyn Botanic Garden, 1993.

————. *Environmental Gardener.* Brooklyn, NY: Brooklyn Botanic Garden, 1992.

————. *Ferns.* Brooklyn, NY: Brooklyn Botanic Garden, 1994.

————. *Gardener's World of Bulbs.* Brooklyn, NY: Brooklyn Botanic Garden, 1991.

————. *Gardening with Wildflowers & Native Plants.* Brooklyn, NY: Brooklyn Botanic Garden, 1962.

————. *Greenhouses & Garden Rooms.* Brooklyn, NY: Brooklyn Botanic Garden, 1990.

———. *Japanese Gardens.* Brooklyn, NY: Brooklyn Botanic Garden, 1990.

———. *Native Perennials.* Brooklyn, NY: Brooklyn Botanic Garden, 1993.

———. *Natural Insect Control.* Brooklyn, NY: Brooklyn Botanic Garden, 1994.

———. *The Natural Lawn & Alternatives.* Brooklyn, NY: Brooklyn Botanic Garden, 1993.

———. *Perennials: A Gardener's Guide.* Brooklyn, NY: Brooklyn Botanic Garden, 1991.

———. *Pruning Techniques.* Brooklyn, NY: Brooklyn Botanic Garden, 1991.

———. *Shrubs.* Brooklyn, NY: Brooklyn Botanic Garden, 1994.

———. *Soils.* Brooklyn, NY: Brooklyn Botanic Garden, 1990.

———. *Woodland Gardens.* Brooklyn, NY: Brooklyn Botanic Garden, 1995.

Editors of Garden Way Publishing. *The Gardener's Complete Q & A.* Pownal, VT: Garden Way Publishing, 1995.

Glattstein, Judy. *Waterscaping: Plants and Ideas for Natural and Created Water Gardens.* Pownal, VT: Storey Publishing, 1994.

Handy, Jenny. *Quick and Easy Topiary and Green Sculpture: Create Traditional Effects with Fast-Growing Climbers and Wire Frames.* Pownal, VT: Storey Publishing, 1996.

Hill, Lewis. *Fruits and Berries for the Home Garden* (Revised and Updated). Pownal, VT: Storey Publishing, 1992.

———. *Pruning Simplified.* Pownal, VT: Garden Way Publishing, 1986.

———. *Secrets of Plant Propagation: Starting Your Own Flowers, Vegetables, Fruits, Berries, Shrubs, Trees, and Houseplants.* Pownal, VT: Storey Publishing, 1985.

Hill, Lewis, and Nancy Hill. *Bulbs: Four Seasons of Beautiful Blooms.* Pownal, VT: Storey Publishing, 1994.

Osborne, Robert A. *Hardy Roses: An Organic Guide to Growing Frost- and Disease-Resistant Varieties.* Pownal, VT: Garden Way Publishing, 1991.

Index

Page references in *italic* indicate illustrations.

Weep holes, 66
Wells, 31
Wet-laid method, 65–66, *65,* 133
Wet wall, 98, *98*
Weyerhauser Corp., 12
Wildflowers, 95–96, *96*
Willingness to pay principle, 11
Wood chip mulch, 101
Woodland plants, 95–96, *96*
Wood structures, questions to ask, 136
World Commission on the Environment and
    Development, 108

X
Xeriscape, 31, 135

Y
Yew plants, 88

Z
"Zaporizhia Oak," 22–23